- *Can't I live a good life without being a Christian?*
- *What about all the suffering in the world?*
- *How can a God of love send people to hell?*
- *Can you prove that Christianity is true?*

Have you ever wrestled with these questions in your own life or stumbled over answers when others asked them? Then you'll appreciate this informative new book. With amusing cartoons and an easy-to-understand style, *If You're There, God, I Have a Few Questions to Ask* provides intellectually sound answers to questions about the Christian faith. Pastor Stephen Gaukroger teaches Bible truths in an intriguing manner and explains why people are afraid of commitment to Jesus Christ. Most important, he proves that Christianity makes sense in our confused world.

Published in Great Britain as *It Makes Sense*, this book was named 1987 Book of the Year by the Christian Booksellers Convention.

Stephen Gaukroger

IF YOU'RE THERE, THERE, GOD, I HAVE A FEW QUESTIONS TO ASK

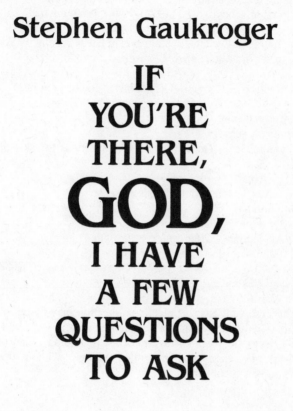

Power Books

Fleming H. Revell
Old Tappan, New Jersey

Unless otherwise identified, Scripture quotations in this volume are from the Good News Bible—Old Testament: Copyright © American Bible Society 1976; New Testament: copyright © American Bible Society 1966, 1971, 1976.

Scripture text identified NIV is from the Holy Bible, New International Version, copyright © 1973, 1978, 1984 International Bible Society. Used by permission of Zondervan Bible Publishers.

This volume was originally published in Great Britain, by Scripture Union, under the title *It Makes Sense*.

Library of Congress Cataloging-in-Publication Data

Gaukroger, Stephen.
    [It makes sense]
    If you're there, God, I have a few questions to ask / Stephen Gaukroger.
        p. cm.
    Previously published as: It makes sense.
    Bibliography: p.
    ISBN 0-8007-5282-1
    1. Apologetics—20th century. I. Title.
BT1102.G34   1987
239—dc19   88-6745
                                                               CIP

Copyright © 1987 by Stephen Gaukroger
Published by the Fleming H. Revell Company
Old Tappan, New Jersey 07675
Printed in the United States of America

Contents

Foreword

For many years, I have been convinced that trends affecting youth are usually seen among British and European young people five to ten years before they are evident in the United States. Stephen Gaukroger's book is immensely popular in England today; therefore, it is my sincere prayer that it will become as popular in the United States.

My reason for this enthusiasm is that the gospel has been presented to youth is an experiential environment for more than a decade. While none would question the value of religious experience, our faith also involves the intellect and the will. This book deals with the common questions that thinking persons have always asked of the Christian faith. The very fact that a book of this type is popular holds out the hope for me that we are beginning to see a shift from what some have quite properly termed "evangelical existentialism" to a faith both biblical and intellectually satisfying as well as emotionally comforting. Very often, today's youth, raised in a sensate environment in which even sound is an emotional-physical stimulant, equate the Christian faith with other mind-altering experiences. Receiving Christ is said to produce a better high than drugs, and a supernatural religious experience is preferred to the educating of the mind and applying oneself to Christian disciplines.

Gaukroger's book is a welcome breath of sound biblical philosophy. His mind is clear, tough, and compassionate. Sooner or later, every person will be driven to ask the questions raised in this book; and unfortunately, if they are not introduced to intellectually and biblically satisfying answers, they will be forced to say, as so many have said, "Hey man, I've been into drugs, I've been into Jesus, I've been into meditation, and none of it works." Jesus as a bromide has never worked; but Jesus Christ as a person, the incarnate Son of God, has never failed. This book deserves a place alongside C. S. Lewis's *Mere Christianity*, Paul Little's *Know What You Believe* and *Know Why You Believe*, and Francis Schaeffer's *The God Who Is There*. This book promises to do for today's youth what these did in former decades.

Neither Gaukroger nor I desire to depreciate legitimate Christian experience, but I think we agree that emotional experience is a result of commitment of the mind and will to a defined, living Christ described in some detail in the Holy Scriptures. This book will help new Christians put a solid foundation under their faith and help them find satisfying answers to the inevitable questions that trouble us all.

Faith is not an intellectual kamikaze or an absence of doubt. Faith is believing and trusting God in the face of bewilderment, anguish, disappointment, and unresolved conflict because "He is" and "is a rewarder of those who diligently seek Him." God has created us and has revealed Himself to us in His Word, His world, and most perfectly in His Son.

Many people today have met people who claim to have "tried Jesus"; however, they have decided, after discussing faith with them, that faith is anti-intellectual and the less sense it makes the better it is. This has caused some of the best potential converts to Christian faith to dismiss Christ without examination. They throw the baby out with the wash water. This book asks us to pause before we do that and seriously examine the claims of Christ and the Bible. It is, therefore, also a book for non-Christians seriously interested in intellectual honesty and unprejudicial exploration of truth.

New Christians should read it, searching non-Christians should give it a try, and witnessing Christians should share it with those with whom they are sharing faith. All will benefit!

JAY KESLER

IF YOU'RE THERE, GOD, I HAVE A FEW QUESTIONS TO ASK

1
Can I really believe in God?

This is the big one. Everything else depends on the answer to this question. Does God exist, or are Christians just imagining the whole thing? And if we end up by proving that God is a figment of our imagination, shouldn't somebody let him know!?

Some people today give the impression that thinking people don't believe in God any more; he has been put in the same category as Father Christmas and the tooth fairy and relegated to 'things we used to believe but have now grown out of'! Well, are Christians just uninformed and gullible people? Or is that perhaps the position of the atheist? Let's try to examine the evidence as honestly as possible.

Atheism

An atheist says that God does not exist. Let's make some observations about this:

It is a statement of faith

Yes, it really is. The atheist can offer no logical, irrefutable proof for his case. He may draw on certain philosophical arguments, personal experiences or 'informed opinion' but in the end none of this will be conclusive proof. Not only that, but the very nature of his case is difficult, as it is always harder to establish clearly what is *not*, than to establish what *is*.

Say, for example, I call downstairs to my wife in the morning telling her that I can't find my socks. She says,

'They're in the spare room.'

I look for a few moments then yell downstairs, 'No they're not!'

'Yes they are,' she replies.

It's much easier for her to prove her case. If she comes upstairs and finds them, she was right. Even if she can't find them straight away, she may still be right if they are found later. To prove my case I have to search every inch of the room, leaving absolutely no space unexplored. She will only have been proved wrong when I have done all this.

Similarly, atheism can only be proved right if every single scrap of information is ferreted out and analysed for traces of God. An impossible task! Not even the most arrogant of human beings would claim to know everything; yet without this knowledge how can the atheist say *for certain* that God does not exist? The statement, 'there is no God' has 'case unproved' stamped across it.

It is very insecure

Being an atheist means living every day with the possibility that evidence will come to light which will prove you wrong. Back to the socks. Every moment of the search could prove me wrong; every moment could prove my wife right. I can only be right at the end of a long search. She could be right any time during the search. This is a trivial illustration, but if the outcome of our search were crucial my every moment would be filled with dread at being proved wrong; hers would be filled with the hope of being proved right. So, logically speaking, an atheist is never secure until he has

explored all the options. George Bernard Shaw, atheist, and brains behind *My Fair Lady*, illustrates how precarious it is:

'The science to which I pinned my faith is bankrupt. I believed it once. In its name I helped destroy the faith of millions of worshippers in the temples of a thousand creeds. And now they look at me and witness the tragedy of an atheist who has lost his faith.'

(G B Shaw, *Too True to be Good*; Constable & Co.)

It is powerless
When was the last time you heard someone say, 'I have just become an atheist and it has turned my life around completely. I used to be an alcoholic who beat my wife, now I have become an ideal family man'? Atheism just doesn't have that kind of moral power. The Christian, on the other hand, can point to dozens of examples of the difference that knowing God has made to people's lives. In the last century an outstanding intellectual named Charles Bradlaugh challenged a local preacher of the gospel to a debate in London. The debate was to compare the claims of Christianity with the claims of atheism. The local minister agreed to the challenge on one condition: that Bradlaugh would bring with him a hundred people whose lives had been changed by their commitment to atheism. If he did so, Hugh Price Hughes would bring a hundred people whose lives had been changed by knowing God. To drive the point home he even offered to debate Bradlaugh if he could bring fifty people who had been changed by their contact with atheism, or twenty, or ten and, eventually, if he could bring *one* man or woman whose life had been changed for the better by contact with atheism. Understandably, Charles Bradlaugh had to withdraw his invitation to debate. Atheism has no moral power to change lives.

In the light of these weaknesses in atheism perhaps we ought to turn our attention to agnosticism.

Agnosticism

An agnostic is someone who says that they don't know whether there is a God or not. Perhaps there is, perhaps there isn't. People often spend quite a long time in this state of 'not knowing' as they struggle to find out about God. Anyone who is genuinely not sure must have our respect but sometimes people are agnostic in a more aggressive sense. It appears in a form like, 'Nobody can be certain about anything, so I'm just not going to commit myself either way.' This person is a permanent agnostic!

However sensible this may seem on the surface, problems appear if we probe a little deeper.

Let's look at the situation logically. Either there is a God or there isn't. One or the other. To the question 'Are you married?' 'Yes' or 'No' are the only two options. 'Possibly' is a nonsense answer! The atheist could be right, those who believe in God could be right . . . the agnostic is bound to be wrong!

People sometimes consider their agnosticism to be intellectually superior to simple Christianity, as if by sitting on the fence they can enjoy the best of both worlds. But being a fence-sitter can be suicidal! Imagine for a moment that you are drowning at sea and two boats arrive to rescue you. They arrive just as you are going down for the third time. You know that one of the boats has a bomb on it and will be blown up within minutes, but you don't know which boat. Because you know only one of the boats can be trusted, you choose to stay in the 'safety' of the water. Sure enough, one of the boats sinks like a stone and the other sails off into the safety of a harbour. You drown! You were so right about only one boat being safe, but so wrong about your decision to stay in the water. Dead wrong! This option was one hundred per cent doomed to failure. At least on the boat you had a fifty/fifty chance of success.

An agnostic is in the same position. Permanently ignoring the only two options, he is condemned to making the wrong choice. Far from being a superior position to hold, it turns out to be the worst of all possible worlds.

And there is more. Many people today reach out for a power beyond themselves. How many of us have half-breathed a prayer to God in the middle of a crisis? The atheist can tell you not to waste your breath. The heavens are empty. Grit your teeth and get on with it. The Christian can say there is help available from a loving God. But the agnostic – he can offer nothing but confusion and doubt! It's as if you are taking a desperately ill friend to hospital in a strange town. 'Where's the hospital?' If someone tells you there isn't one you are upset but resigned to the fact that there's nothing more you can do. If someone tells you there is a hospital and where it is, you race there happily to get help for your friend. If someone tells you there may well be a hospital but that they have never heard of it, nor do they know where it is if there is one . . . this is maddeningly frustrating! A glimmer of hope but no way to reach it. 'Thanks for nothing', you think.

We are beginning to see that this 'not knowing' isn't half as clever as it is made out to be. As a point on the road to discovery it is perfectly sensible; as a settled opinion it is wrong, dangerous and of no help to others. Agnosticism is like the Mersey Tunnel – all right to travel through, but a nightmare to live in!

Clues to God's existence

No one can prove the existence of God! But in a way that's not surprising; absolutely conclusive proof about anything is very difficult to find. I am sure my wife loves me. I am sure of this because she says so, does loving things and never gives me reason to doubt her. I don't however, have any concrete proof. It is possible that she is just a superb actress and is patiently waiting for the best opportunity to smother me in my sleep and claim the insurance!

So what follows is not so much proof, as a series of indications that God exists; pointers in his direction. As if a thief had broken into your house, burgled your home, but been clumsy enough to leave his gloves off. When you arrive home things may appear in disarray but a closer examination reveals finger prints, and clues to the thief's identity. All over our world God has left his finger prints, divine clues as to his existence and identity.

Clue 1: The exploding supermarket
The first clue in the search to discover whether God exists is found in the remarkable order and design in the universe. Things seem to fit together in an amazing way. Let's look at some examples.

If the earth were smaller than it is (or larger) it would not be able to sustain an atmosphere we could breathe. If it were a jot nearer the sun we would fry, or a whisker further away and we would freeze. If the earth spun more slowly, if it were tilted at a different angle, if the moon were nearer, if the ozone layer which surrounds the earth were thinner . . . any one of these things would spell disaster for our planet. Yet each one of them stays in harmony with the others to enable life on earth to continue.

And what about human life itself? Plants produce oxygen which we need; we produce carbon dioxide which plants need. Now there's a clever arrangement. Every cell in the human body has the same number of chromosomes – apart, that is, from those which join together to form a new human being. They have exactly half that number so that when they join with a similar cell from someone else they have the right number again. From this single cell fingers, legs, hair, skin, blood, etc. are formed; not to mention all the intricate workings of the brain, heart and other organs!

Our lives and our universe seem to have a unique designer label – God. What else accounts for this precision handiwork? Chance? Fate? Surely not. That's as hard to believe as an explosion in a supermarket accidently producing a Christmas dinner with all the trimmings!

Sir Isaac Newton, one of the great scientists of the seventeenth century, once built a model of the solar system to help him in his studies. One of his atheistic scientist friends came to see him one day and asked who made the model. 'Nobody!' Newton replied. When the scientist accused him of being ridiculous, Newton explained that if no one had a problem in realizing that a model needed a maker, why was it such a problem when confronted with the real universe?

What Isaac Newton was driving at was that we all take for granted that the many objects we see about us had a designer and builder. However, we seem able to believe that the greatest objects, the world and life itself, just happened. This does seem to be incredibly inconsistent. Isn't it more reasonable to assume that all this order and design in our universe happened because there is a great designer?

Clue 2: A hole in the middle
The second clue is found in ourselves and our desires and needs. We all have basic drives and instincts which need to be fulfilled. We get hungry, thirsty and cold from time to time and, when we do, we try to meet those needs. A Big Mac for the hunger, a Pepsi to satisfy our thirst and thermal underwear for the cold! All these basic desires have a corresponding fulfilment. Just imagine how awful life would be if there was no way for these inner needs to be met. If we had to spend our entire life feeling cold; if we felt desperately tired but there was no such thing as sleep . . . it begins to sound like hell itself! All these deep inner needs have their corresponding fulfilment beyond ourselves: food meets the need called hunger, drink meets the need called thirst, and so on.

What meets man's basic need to worship? It is hard to find a race of people who don't have this desire in some form or other. Search as we may among primitive tribes, we keep coming up with belief in some kind of God or gods: some force greater than ourselves worthy of our worship. Or what about the 'civilized' world? Perhaps we know better than those 'ignorant savages' and don't feel the need to worship, to acknowledge anything greater than ourselves. But if we go to Hollywood, and its difficult to get more sophisticated than that, we find a group of women who have all been married to famous celebrities, formed into a group called LADIES – Life After Divorce Is Eventually Sane. They begin their meetings with a 'spiritual', a time to focus on some force or power outside themselves. So much for sophisticated people not having a need to worship something!

This need is found in every continent and in every country, among millions of ordinary, educated people, and is acknowledged by all the world's major religions and new religious movements. All this is true despite opposition to religion – Communists ban it, atheists reject it, dictators abuse it, intellectuals scoff at it and governments suppress it. Yet here we are, near the end of the twentieth century, and religious life of all kinds continues to flourish on our planet! There does seem to be a worldwide desire to worship something. Now if all the needs we mentioned earlier had a corresponding fulfilment, doesn't it seem reasonable that the need to worship would also have a corresponding fulfilment? In other words, is there a God who meets the need for worship? If there is no God, this need is the only one of all our needs to which there is no solution.

If we think about our own experience we sense that this may be true. A fleeting feeling that there must be more to life than appears on the surface; a half curse, half prayer shouted at God in a crisis; the thought of being reunited with someone you love as you stand at their graveside. All these are indications that in our innermost being we cry out for something greater than ourselves. Pascal, a seventeenth-century philosopher and mathematician, said that inside every person there is a God-shaped vacuum; a sort of hole in the middle of our beings. We have, he said, a need that only God can meet. All the indications are that he was right!

Clue 3: Mugging rules OK?
The fact that we know right from wrong points to the existence of God. Most of us have a remarkable amount in common in this area. We agree that killing someone is wrong. We have no hesitation in condemning dishonesty, greed and selfishness, along with rape and mugging. Now we may still do some of these things ourselves, but we know the standards exist and certainly expect other people to abide by them!

Even our daily conversation betrays our belief in values or standards to which we ought to conform. 'I ought to visit my elderly mother.' 'How could they do that to the child?' 'It's disgusting what young people get up to these days!' But where do these values come from? If the atheist is right, why should we care about these values? If there is no God then we have no Power to be responsible to, and anything goes! Yet this kind of society is impossible to imagine – one in which betraying your friends, sexually assaulting your children or mugging old ladies is perfectly reasonable.

So where do these standards come from? Some have argued that each society decides what's right for itself. But a close look at the history of some of the world's most famous societies shows a remarkable agreement between them. The Egyptian, Roman, Greek and ancient Chinese cultures have major areas of agreement with our own. Far from setting their own standards they all appear to be conforming to an objective standard beyond each of them. For centuries people have tried to come up with alternatives to God as the source of our standards – none of the alternatives comes close to explaining the facts.

What is incredible is that some people in our society write God off and still maintain their values. If we are all here by accident and are subject to chance throughout our lives, only eventually to die with no hope of a future, who cares about standards and values! If we are just advanced animals, let's behave like animals! But no society lives like this. Our values must have come from somewhere. It is at least reasonable to believe they came from a moral, wise mind. Christians call this mind, God.

Clue 4: A cosmic ERNIE

What is the purpose of life? Why are we here? What does it all mean? If there is no God, the human race just happened, evolving by chance from some primeval slime. We are just a random collection of atoms flung together over millions of years, finally becoming human. A huge accident. We are just premium bond numbers spat out at random by a cosmic ERNIE – the whole of our lives, our very existence, one gigantic fluke.

Serious atheists down the centuries have expressed this

meaninglessness which, they have to agree, is the logical conclusion of their atheism. Listen to the utter hopelessness of Baron Montesquieu, an eighteenth-century philosopher: 'We should weep for men at their birth, not at their death.' Why? Because life is meaningless and so we should pity everyone who has to go through this experience. Feel the sense of futility and uselessness from Mark Twain, nearing the end of his life:

'Men are born, they labour and sweat and struggle; they squabble and scold and fight; those they love are taken from them, and the joy of life is turned to aching grief. The release comes at last and they vanish from a world where they were of no consequence . . . a world which will lament them a day and forget them forever.'

Or a twentieth-century philosopher, Albert Camus, saying, 'What is intolerable is to see one's life drained of meaning. To be told that there is no reason for existing. A man can't live without some reason for living.' Or Jean-Paul Sartre, 'This world is not the product of intelligence. It meets our gaze as would a crumpled piece of paper . . . what is man but a little puddle of water whose freedom is death?' And see the effect of this hopelessness on Friedrich Nietzsche, spending the last ten years of his life in a lunatic asylum. His biographer says that this was partly the result of trying to live with the logic of his position as an atheist!

All these men saw that the strictly logical conclusion to draw from their atheism was that life was absurd and meaningless. The fact is, however, that thousands of atheists don't want to face the logic of this because it is too painful; thousands of others live in ignorance of their true position. It's as if a fish denied the existence of water while continuing to swim in it and to feed on other life growing there. Many atheists want to reject God but hold on to what a belief in God provides – meaning and purpose! Your average atheist lives his entire life without being aware of this depressing consequence of atheism. If he were aware of it, the purposelessness would overwhelm him. Human life cries out for fulfilment. Belief in God provides us with the possibility of an explanation for our existence, a sense of destiny about our future and a reason for living today. Atheism is a broken, empty philosophy in comparison.

Clue 5: Who dunnit?

Sometimes, my wife and I have disagreements. Something has been left on the living-room floor – a mug of half drunk tea, a newspaper or a set of keys. (There now follows a dramatic dialogue.) Wife tidying up . . .

Wife: Who put that there?
Me: Don't look at me!
Wife: I am looking at you!
Me: I didn't put it there!
Wife: Who else could have?!
Me: Perhaps you did!!
Wife: Don't be ridiculous!!!
(Exit all)

Now the point which our minor domestic tiff illustrates is this. Despite the disagreement there is one thing on which we are absolutely united. *Somebody* left it there. Who dunnit? Somebody did. It didn't appear by magic. If we didn't agree on this simple fact we would have no basis on which to argue. The principle we are operating on is this – everything is caused by something else. The paper this book is written on came from a tree which came from a seed which came from . . . and so on. I came into being through my parents and they, would you believe, came into being through their parents. Nothing in our lives just 'happened' or started without something making it happen.

We are forced to ask what it was that started the whole thing off in the very beginning. You might say it was chance or fate; but that doesn't really help us. Chance or luck is not the *cause* of anything, just a description of events for which we can't find an adequate cause or reason. For example, if a 200–to–1–against horse, with a limp and one blind eye, wins the Grand National we would describe that as lucky or a fluke. But this 'chance' element didn't cause the horse to win. It merely describes the fact that we can't explain how it won. So to say that the universe started by chance is just like saying that it started, but we don't know how.

This brings us to the other alternative – God started it. This is a reasonable possibility and stands up well to the other options. 'This world is here because someone put it here' is a statement to be taken very seriously.

Clue 6: Pleased to meet you

Thousands and thousands of people claim to have met him—God, that is. They say that he has changed their lives. Without giving it more than a few seconds' thought I can think of doctors, bricklayers, lawyers, housewives, secretaries, teachers and groundsmen who could talk about meeting God. There are pensioners, children and every age in between. People from Asia, Africa and America; black people and white people; and these are just some of those known to me personally! It's very difficult indeed to write off all these people as cranks, unintelligent or gullible. So what is it that has changed their lives? A belief that there really is a God who can be met and who changes lives.

All six of these clues ought to be examined seriously. Each clue points to the existence of God; together they present a strong case which we must face honestly. If you can say that you are certain there is no God, read no further. If you are willing to admit the possibility of God's existence, but still have further questions, read on!

2
What about all the suffering?

'I was only ten years old when death first struck my own family. My father died just hours before I returned home from a term at a British boarding school. As I neared my house I could hear weeping. I ran through the gate and was in the door before my mother even knew I was back. Tears filled my eyes when I saw my father's dead body.

I felt completely devastated by my father's death. I was angry at everything and everyone. "It isn't fair" I thought. "Why couldn't my dad die in old age like other dads?" '
(Luis Palau, *Tough Questions*; Hodder and Stoughton.)

It would take a cold, hard person not to share some of Argentinian Luis Palau's heartache. Many of us have asked similar questions – why did my mother die of cancer? Why was my best friend paralysed in a car accident? Why are so many people starving to death? The question of suffering boils down to this: How can a God of love let all this suffering go on in his world? Either he doesn't exist at all or he is a vicious tyrant who enjoys seeing people in pain! This seems a pretty strong case against the existence of a loving God and there certainly is no slick or easy answer to the problem of suffering. But it is like a child's jigsaw puzzle, with large pieces that fit together to make a picture;

if we take one piece at a time the child begins to overcome its confusion and starts to see how the whole picture fits together. Our confusion at this massive puzzle (how can a loving, powerful God stand by while we suffer?) will become clearer if we take it one piece at a time.

Jigsaw piece 1

For much of the suffering in our world we only have ourselves to blame. It's no good blaming God when a drunken driver kills an innocent pedestrian or when a football hooligan knifes one of your friends on the way home from the match! Both these incidents, and thousands like them, point the finger at the real culprits – the human race. God can hardly be blamed for the sufferings we as a race choose to bring on ourselves. When nations hoard food and refuse aid to the hungry, when governments declare war on each other, when gangs terrorize housing estates, when adults sexually abuse children, when old people are robbed and beaten, *we* are to blame.

Now it's true that we *personally* may not be to blame for all these problems. But we *are* personally to blame for some things. No one reading this book can honestly say they have never caused anyone any suffering. Never an angry word to your husband or child? A selfish action at work? A refusal to help someone in need? No, the plain fact is that, to a greater or lesser degree, we all contribute to the suffering in the world. This was illustrated by the response to a competition in a national newspaper. Readers were asked to write on the theme, 'What's wrong with the world?' From thousands of entries the winner was a man whose letter was also the briefest:

'Dear Sir, I am, Yours faithfully.'

So, God could only get rid of the suffering we inflict on ourselves by getting rid of us (pretty drastic!) or by making us into robots who only acted on his command. Both these options would rob us of our freedom of choice. Having been given the privilege of free will, we have to live with the consequences of our choices. Both suffering and joy come from these choices.

Some people argue that there is a further option. Why can't God stop the actions of bad men? To do that, he would have to intervene in our affairs all the time, changing the laws of nature. A bullet from a bad man's gun could turn into a feather if aimed at someone; a mugger's knife could become a banana as it was about to strike. But it is impossible to imagine a world like this. Without consistent laws we would never know where we were – life would be a nightmare of confusion and unpredictability. Compare it to playing tennis with a friend. If he persistently double faults, you may, to be kind, allow him another service. If he trips, you may agree to play the point again. But if you ignore the lines and the net completely, you are simply not playing tennis. It has become a different game altogether.

So it is with God in our world. He can intervene from time to time but basically he has to uphold the laws of the 'game'. Without these dependable rules we could not exist at all. This means, sadly, that whether a knife is stuck into wood or human flesh – damage is the consequence.

Jigsaw piece 2

What about all the suffering we don't cause, the things we have no control over? Like earthquakes, famine, volcanoes and other natural disasters. Strange as it may seem, we must take some responsibility even for the suffering caused by natural disasters.

Earthquakes, for instance, have caused death, homelessness and injury on a huge scale. Thousands suffered in Algeria in 1980 and in Mexico in 1985 – to name two recent examples. What is not as well known is that vast amounts of this suffering could have been prevented. As long ago as 1906 earthquakes were monitored and the resulting devastation scrutinized. Dr T Nakamura was sent by the

Japanese Government to San Francisco after the earthquake there to assess why there had been such colossal loss of life, injury and devastation. In his report this sentence stands out: 'Dishonest mortar was responsible for nearly all the earthquake damage.' In other words the damage could have been drastically reduced by decent, reinforced buildings! Twenty-nine years later, in 1935, we read this report in *The Times* after a major earthquake in Pakistan:

'The appalling destruction in Quetta City is traced to the poor constructional quality of the buildings. Such earthquake-proof buildings as had been built in the area survived the catastrophe. Not even their chimneys fell.'

What is absolutely staggering is that the same newspaper, *The Times*, wrote after the Mexican earthquake on October 8th 1985 that among the reasons for the disaster were,

' . . . second-rate workmanship and skimping on construction materials. There is wide agreement that many buildings need not have fallen, and that many lives could have been saved had some builders been more scrupulous. Probably the strongest lesson from the Mexico City disaster is that good architecture works.'

In other words over fifty years ago we knew how to minimize earthquake damage; events in Mexico have revealed how little we have put this knowledge into practice. No wonder the song writer asks 'when will they ever learn?'

And there is a human dimension to other natural disasters. For example, thousands suffered and died during the Ethiopian famine of 1985. But did you know that two years before it happened relief organizations had warned governments that it was coming? And that the Ethiopian Government was spending millions on lavish premises in Addis Ababa while, less than 200 miles away, people starved? A great deal of pain could have been avoided by governments and individuals acting in a different way.

It does seem unreasonable to blame God for our own

unwillingness as a race to act. Think of disaster after disaster in this country – almost without exception there is human failure which either caused the catastrophe or made it considerably worse. We do have to carry the can for some of this responsibility ourselves.

Having said all this, there is some suffering which appears to be beyond our control; natural disasters which strike without warning and seemingly without cause. How can we explain this?

Christians believe that God made a perfect world. Unfortunately, man decided he knew better than God about how things ought to be run, and turned his back on God. This resulted in a rift between God and man which also affected the world about him. A once perfect world became imperfect; man found himself in alien territory surrounded by a natural world which was now 'red in tooth and claw'; a world infected by sickness and disease. (You can read the full story in the Bible; the first three chapters.) So the environment we live in is often hostile; Christians see this as a result of man's revolt.

Jigsaw piece 3

This is quite a small piece of the jigsaw really, but it's the one we feel most – pain! We tend to take this aspect of suffering very personally! If we, or a close friend, endure long periods of pain, we tend to get angry with God for letting the suffering go on. But if God were to remove pain completely it would be disastrous for us as humans. Our appendix could burst with no warning; our teeth could go rotten and we would never know; we could lose whole limbs in a fire without realizing it. When you go to the doctor he asks you where the pain is – this helps him locate the problem and attempt a diagnosis and cure. Without the pain his job would be much more difficult! Pain, far from being an enemy, can be a friend. It is the body's early warning system. Without it, life would be unimaginably worse than it is now. Doctor Paul Brand, a leading specialist in the study of pain, has researched for years into the reasons for pain, particularly in connection with the disease leprosy. He recounts incident after tragic incident of patients who have lost all sensation of pain in one or more limbs – hands cut to the bone during routine domestic jobs, fingers bitten right off, toes severed while a patient was digging a garden – all without any realization of what was happening. No wonder Doctor Brand can say, 'Thank God for inventing pain. I don't think he could have done a better job.'

Perhaps we should pause for a moment to see how far we have come in piecing together the great puzzle of suffering. We have admitted that the human race brings a great deal of suffering on itself and could do a great deal more to alleviate the suffering there is. We have seen that we live in an imperfect natural world which is potentially hostile to us. As long as we have freedom of choice, some of us will choose to cause suffering. And pain is not the great enemy it often appears to be.

Now we must be absolutely honest and say that all this still leaves us with large gaps in our jigsaw. None of the explanations we have discussed is fully satisfying when faced with a badly deformed baby, a major plane disaster or a horribly disfigured accident victim. No one, anywhere in the world, has a totally convincing answer to the problem of suffering. But Christians have two more pieces of the jigsaw to help us come to terms with the situation.

Jigsaw piece 4

God understands our suffering because he has experienced it! Let no one accuse God of being an uninvolved deity, just sitting back and watching us suffer. He sent his son to earth to check it out for himself, to experience first-hand what life was all about for us humans. A piece called *The long silence* sums this up more powerfully than any other words I can use.

At the end of time, billions of people were scattered on a great plain before God's throne. Most shrank back from the brilliant light before them. But some groups near the front talked heatedly – not with cringing shame but with belligerence. 'Can God judge us?'

'How can He know about suffering?' snapped a pert young brunette. She ripped open a sleeve to reveal a tattooed number from a Nazi concentration camp. 'We endured terror . . . beating . . . torture . . . death!'

In another group a Negro boy lowered his collar. 'What about this?' he demanded, showing an ugly rope burn. 'Lynched for no crime but being black!'

In another crowd, a pregnant school girl with sullen eyes. 'Why should I suffer?' she murmured. 'It wasn't my fault.'

Far out across the plain were hundreds of such groups. Each had a complaint against God for the evil and suffering He permitted in His world. How lucky God was to live in heaven where all was sweetness and light, where there was no weeping or fear, no hunger or hatred. What did God know of all that men had been forced to endure in this world? For God leads a pretty sheltered life, they said.

So each of these groups sent forth their leader, chosen because he had suffered the most. A Jew, a Negro, a person from Hiroshima, a horribly deformed arthritic, a thalidomide child. In the centre of the plain they consulted with each other.

At last they were ready to present their case. It was rather clever. Before God could be qualified to be their judge, He must endure what they had endured. Their verdict was that God should be sentenced to live on earth – as a man! Let him be born a Jew. Let the legitimacy of His birth be doubted. Give Him a work so difficult that even His family will think Him out of His mind when He tries to do it. Let Him be betrayed by His closest friends. Let Him face false charges, be tried by a prejudiced jury and convicted by a cowardly judge. Let Him be tortured. At last, let Him see what it means to be terribly alone. Then let Him die. Let Him die so that there can be no doubt He died. Let there be a whole host of witnesses to verify it.

As each leader announced his portion of the sentence, loud murmurs of approval went up from the throng of people assembled. When the last had finished pronouncing sentence there was a long silence. No one uttered another word. No one moved. For suddenly all knew that God had already served His sentence.

Many people find great comfort and help from this knowledge – God has felt our pain and he understands. He has been where we are: the boss has been on the shop floor, the captain has worked in the engine room, the chief of police has walked the beat. God has been down at the sharp end, right where we are. Dorothy Sayers summarizes the whole thing when she says,

'For whatever reason God chose to make man as he is – limited and suffering and subject to sorrows and death – He had the honesty and the courage to take His own medicine. Whatever game He is playing with His creation He has kept His own rules and played fair. He has Himself gone through the whole of human experience, from the trivial irritations of family life and lack of money to the worst horrors, pain, humiliation, defeat, despair and death. He was born in poverty and died in disgrace and felt it well worthwhile.'

(Dorothy Sayers, *The Man Born to be King*; Gollancz.)

Jigsaw piece 5

The best cure for a bleeding wound is a bandage, not a talk about suffering! For most of us when we are suffering, what we want is not clever answers to philosophical questions but practical, down-to-earth, help. If we deny the existence of a loving God (by saying he is a figment of our imagination or by saying he exists but won't come to our rescue) we rob ourselves of the major source of help. If there is no God, all that happens is a result of chance – not much comfort there! If he just doesn't care – that's even worse! What an awful position to be in.

In contrast, Christians believe in a God who can help. Despite many misunderstandings Christianity is not pie in the sky when you die; it's steak on the plate while you wait! It's about a relationship with someone who is with us in every difficulty and who promises never to leave us however tough it gets. This story, called simply, *Footprints*, illustrates God's help for Christians as they struggle with suffering.

One night a man had a dream. He dreamed he was walking along the beach with the Lord and across the sky flashed scenes from his life. For each scene, he noticed two sets of footprints in the sand; one belonging to him and the other to the Lord.

When the last scene of his life flashed before him, he looked back at the footprints in the sand. He noticed that many times along the path of his life there was only one set of footprints. He also noticed that it happened at the very lowest and saddest times in his life.

This really bothered him and he questioned the Lord about it, 'Lord, you said that once I decided to follow you, you'd walk with me all the way. But I have noticed that during the most troublesome times in my life, there is only one set of footprints. I don't understand why when I needed you most, you would leave me.'

The Lord replied, 'My precious, precious child, I love you and I would never leave you. During your times of trial and suffering, when you see only one set of footprints, it was then that I carried you.'

This kind of help is not that easy to beat! Along with it goes a guarantee to every Christian that all his unanswered questions will one day have answers, all the wrongs will be put to right, and he will have for ever to enjoy a life without suffering of any kind. This expectation has strengthened and encouraged Christians over the centuries. It sounds like a fantastic offer, and it is. Be careful not to reject this as a fairy story too quickly – if you dismiss it without thought, just think what an idiot you would feel one second after you die to discover it was true!

What it adds up to is this: there is a tremendous amount of pain in individual lives. We have been given an offer of help and support in this life and a complete absence of suffering in the next. There is not much else on offer so we might as well check it out pretty carefully.

Many thinkers have given their own hints as to why suffering is allowed in our world. C S Lewis can say, 'God whispers to us in our pleasures, speaks in our conscience, but shouts in our pain: it is His megaphone to rouse a deaf world.' So suffering is used by God to act as a global conscience, focusing our attention on life's vital issues. Alexander Solzhenitsyn's own experience of suffering taught him things about himself and he came to be grateful for it. 'It was only when I lay there on rotting prison straw that I sensed within myself the first stirrings of good. So, bless you, prison, for having been in my life.'

Wherever we are, bad experiences can teach us many things and we can agree that we would have been worse as people without them. Let's admit though, that even with all the pieces in this chapter, the jigsaw is still incomplete. Although Christians have some extra pieces, honesty compels us to admit that we have not got to the bottom of the problem of suffering. To some extent we are all in a fog about this; blindly groping our way towards our destiny. The major difference is that the Christian can see a dim light in the distance drawing him on, others must struggle with the same fog but with an ever deeper blackness beyond.

3
What about the other religions?

Thirty years ago few people in the western world would have thought this a very important question. Now, towards the end of the twentieth century, we are all aware of the faiths which vie for our attention. The age of the jet plane has made rapid movement possible all over our planet. The Sikh family we used to read about in our school text books now lives next door. TV exposes us to the whole gamut of world religions and, suddenly, our cosy little world is shattered by the insight that not everyone thinks, believes or acts like we do.

Of every six people in the world, one is a Moslem. Add to these the followers of Confucius and adherents to Buddhism and Hinduism, and you end up with about forty per cent of the world's population. No wonder Christians are often asked, 'What about all these other religions?'

Surely Christianity is not saying almost half the population of the world has got it wrong? Isn't it arrogant to believe that Christians are the only ones who have got it right?

Is sincerity enough?

In conversation with people who are not committed Christians I have been told: 'I think genuine followers of all religions will get there in the end; God wouldn't reject anyone who was sincere.' On the surface this seems a perfectly reasonable statement, and a very attractive one as well because it credits God with generosity, and us with tolerance. It also means there's no need to work hard to examine the evidence and discover the truth. I can believe what I want as long as I am sincere. Despite this I am afraid that we are going to reject the sincerity option for two reasons.

First, it's wrong.

Sincerity is not enough. Hitler may have been completely sincere in his desire to eliminate the Jews and create a super race. But very few people would say that the slaughter of six million Jews was right! The best we can say for Hitler is that he was sincerely wrong.

And what about you and me? We may sincerely believe that Dallas is in Africa, that the moon is made of cheese or that a Mars Bar is a pub on another planet! But we would be wrong. Nobody is going to be impressed if, having heard all the scientific evidence to the contrary, we persist in saying 'but I *sincerely* believe the moon is made of cheese!' And what if *millions* sincerely believed that the earth, for example, was flat? They did once, and they were wrong! Sincerity can't make wrong facts right.

However hard you think, it is impossible to come up with an everyday example which supports the theory that all you need is sincerity. We just don't live like that; it wouldn't work.

Secondly, it's dangerous.
Imagine that you have a very young child who suddenly comes out in a rash. A friend who happens to be visiting you says there is nothing to worry about, her daughter had the same rash when she was a baby. 'It goes away in a couple of weeks' you are assured. Ten days later your child is rushed into hospital, its life only just saved by a skilful doctor. What went wrong? A well-meaning friend has misled you. The rash looked the same, but it wasn't. Her sincerity is not in question, she genuinely wanted to help; but her advice turned out to be wrong. This kind of sincerity can be fatal! What you and your young child needed most was not a sincere diagnosis but an accurate one!

All this is even more crucial in matters of religious belief. Christians maintain that our personal destiny is at stake here; get these facts wrong and we could miss out on real fulfilment now and life with God for ever when we die.

What we need desperately is not a sincere view of God but an accurate one. There is nothing more tragic than committing yourself to a system of beliefs or a life-style which is ultimately futile. It would be like spending a lifetime climbing a ladder only to discover at the top that it is leaning against the wrong wall!

So we are forced to conclude that even if you are the most sincere person in the world you could still be wrong. To be sincere is not enough.

Two Misunderstandings

Before we examine the claim that Christianity is unique, let's try to clear up two popular misunderstandings. Both seem extremely plausible but, in reality, are like the house fronts on a Hollywood set – when you look behind them there's nothing there!

'All roads lead to God'

This view holds that whatever faith or religious outlook you have, everyone ends up at the same place. Different religions are just different routes to the same destination, so it doesn't really matter which one you believe.

Does this argument hold water? Are people really saying that all religious beliefs, from every culture in the world, from all the years of history, and all the new religious movements in the future, are all leading to God? How can that be when so many different things are believed, many of which are the exact opposite of somebody else's belief? For example, some people believe that their God is pleased by human sacrifices; others believe that their God is appalled by them – they are not worshipping the same God! Such is the variety of religious belief that you might as well say it doesn't matter what you believe as long as you are sincere! No, I'm afraid this option just doesn't add up.

What if we say that it is only the major world religions that lead to God? There is of course a massive problem here – which religions are major? Which should be left out?

What criteria shall we use to decide? Even if we take the five most commonly thought of as the world's major religions, a brief examination reveals mammoth differences between them. Hinduism believes in many gods; Islam is absolutely insistent that there is only one. Buddhism is silent about the nature, or even existence of God; Judaism describes his character in detail. Christians believe in one life and death for each individual; Buddhists believe in multiple reincarnations.

And what about the way of salvation, the way to eternal life? Many ancient religions offer salvation through gifts and offerings to the gods, even human sacrifices. In Hinduism we discover that fulfilment of duty, ceremonial observance and discipline lead to salvation. Muslims must fulfil their obligations to fast and pray, and recite their creed. Then, although they may taste judgment, they will eventually enter paradise. Christians, in opposition to all the others, say salvation can't be earned by doing anything; you receive it as a gift.

In other words, the world's major religions are not going in the same direction or to the same destination. It's only possible to believe that 'all roads lead to God' if we remain ignorant about these different religions (the roads) and their view of God (the destination). All religions do not lead to the same point any more than all planes from Heathrow go to New York or all roads from Luton lead to London!

Sometimes, even people who know a little about the world's religions have a very hazy, sentimental view of the way they fit together. They think that God is something like a huge painting. Each religion completes one part of the picture and so, it is said, each of them is true . . . just not the whole story. God (the painting) is big enough to contain all their views and ideas. The reality is that the world's religions are not just different but *contradictory*. Hindus would say there are several paintings, all different; Muslims would say there was one painting. Buddhists would say that the painting was irrelevant, therefore the frame was probably empty. Christians would say that there were three distinct aspects to the painting, but all in the one frame. *Somebody is wrong.* To say that 'all roads lead to God' is as illogical as saying that a bike ride to school is no different from a rocket ride to the moon. The route, mode of transport and destination are all completely different!

'I'm sure it helps you'

Probably never before has there been so much to choose from. In almost every sphere of life the number and variety of options is becoming immense. Selling techniques major on the fact that product X may be all right for others, but product Y is what *you* and your family really need. Try asking for a pain-killer in the chemist. Liquid or pill? Aspirin or Paracetamol? Tablet or capsule? Name brand or chemist's own? Extra strength? Small or large packet? It's enough to *give* you a headache!

As new religious movements have sprung up and old ones have become better known in America and Britain, the 'customer is king' mentality has begun to infiltrate even the area of belief. We can accept new religions with all the indifference with which we greet a new supermarket chain. 'He is a Hindu and I am a Christian' is seen as little more than an accident of birth, taste and culture. 'He has chosen Hinduism, that's fine for him; I have chosen Christianity and that suits me' – as if the choice is as insignificant as saying 'he shops at Sainsburys, that's fine for him; I shop at Safeway and that suits me.'

Now it's true that in the religious supermarket we do have a choice. The difference is that the choice has far-reaching implications because these products are very different and their effect on our lives is total. This is because a belief is either true for everybody or nobody. Christianity is more like gravity than stamp collecting: a fact rather than an option. There is no middle ground here; either Christianity is true – whether or not we believe it – or it isn't. To say that it is all right for someone else but not for you is both patronizing and wrong. The Christian faith claims to open the way to God and give some answers to profound questions about life and death. These answers are either right (for everybody) or wrong (for everybody).

Let's now move on to examine why Christianity claims to be unique, and whether these claims stand up to scrutiny.

Christianity *claims* to be unique

There is little doubt about what Christianity claims for itself. Here are two quotations from the Bible, the Christian's manual of faith:

'I am the way, the truth and the life; no one goes to the Father except by me.'[1]

'Salvation is to be found through him [Jesus] alone; in all the world there is no one else whom God has given who can save us.'[2]

Both these statements indicate the exclusiveness of Christianity. Faith in Jesus is seen as the only way to find God. No amount of fudging can remove the clear thrust of statements like these.

At first glance this seems harsh and unbending, even incredibly arrogant! But if you think about it, isn't all truth ultimately like this? Two plus two equals four. I may want it to equal five, or seven, or even seventy-seven, but the fact is that the answer is four. Five might seem near enough, but actually it has more in common with a thousand – both are wrong! In practice we *expect* the truth to be exclusive; excluding what is wrong. Christianity claims to be *the* truth about the way to God; the nature of this claim makes it impossible to reconcile it with other religions. They may contain truth but only Christianity is the whole truth.

In contrast to this, other religions have an inclusiveness which is superficially attractive. Most of them can absorb Jesus and his teachings under their general umbrella. Hinduism, in particular, has room for Jesus among its many gods. But it's this very inclusiveness which should worry a determined seeker after truth. Let's go back to the arithmetic to illustrate this. Two plus two equals:

Truth	Error
4	5 or 7 or 11 or 2,476,312 etc., etc.

Notice that by its very nature error is more inclusive than truth. In this case it is able to include absolutely every number other than four! This tends to suggest that the very inclusiveness which is claimed to be enlightened or tolerant by many religious movements turns out to be just plain error wearing a fancy hat! Christianity's very exclusiveness is an indication that it may be the truth.

Perhaps we ought to pause for a moment here to clarify what Christianity is not saying. It is not saying that all the teaching in every other religion is completely wrong. Many of the things they teach are morally uplifting and promote high ethical standards. Neither are genuine Christians looking down on other people who have different beliefs, with a dismissive arrogance or superior attitude. Our position as Christians is simply this. We have been faced with an ultimatum from God: 'Come to me on the basis of my son's death for you. That's the way, take it or leave it.' We decided that we would come and are thrilled that we did. *We* did not make Christianity exclusive and we cannot change it any more than we can change the law of gravity. We, along with the rest of the human race, are faced with a choice – am I going to accept that this exclusive claim is true? Yes or no. Our destiny will be decided by the answer!

Christianity *is* unique

We have seen that Christianity claims to be unique. But how is this uniqueness seen in practice? Let's consider some of the main differences between being a Christian and following another religion.

Salvation is not earned

All religions, other than Christianity, have a kind of points system for obtaining eternal life. Hindus must live to the best of their ability, not hurting even the lowliest of animals, in order to achieve a better kind of life next time round. If they live bad lives they may be reincarnated to a more destitute human existence or even come back as an insect. Muslims must fulfil a number of obligations if they are to receive salvation. They must abstain from alcohol, make a pilgrimage to Mecca, fast during the month of Ramadhan and pray five times a day. Buddhists must strive to overcome desire if they want to obtain salvation. Each religious movement has its own rules to follow if you are to be acceptable to God. This is where Christianity is completely different. Let's look at the manual again:

' . . . God's free gift is eternal life in union with Christ Jesus our Lord.'[3]

'For it is by God's grace that you have been saved through faith. It is not the result of your own efforts, but God's gift, so that no one can boast about it.'[4]

The Christian faith says that the points system doesn't work; no one has ever accumulated enough to pass heaven's entrance exam. The kindest, nicest person on the face of the earth still fails to achieve the pass mark: perfection. There is, in fact, a one hundred per cent failure rate. So far so bad! The good news is that Jesus lived a perfect life and became the only person ever to make the grade. God then says to a world of exam failures that as a graduation present for his son he would like to offer us salvation (eternal life in heaven and his presence with us now) as a free gift. Not on the basis of what we have earned, or what we deserve, but because of what his son has accomplished. Unlike other religions we can do absolutely nothing to work for salvation; we must just receive it as a free gift.

'But Christianity *does* have rules and regulations like any other faith – what about going to church and loving your neighbour and not committing adultery?!' Yes, it's true that there are rules to follow in Christianity, but they are of a totally different kind. Put briefly, they are a *result* of our salvation not the cause of it. It's a little like my relationship with my wife. I try to show my love to her by helping with Bethany (our young daughter), doing some jobs about the house and buying the occasional bunch of flowers. None of this is to win her love – she already loves me. In fact a diamond necklace and a Rolls Royce would not make her love me if she had not chosen to do so already. In a similar way, no amount of effort on my part will earn God's love, but because he already loves me I want to express my gratitude by following his rules. This makes the Christian faith fundamentally different from other viewpoints. They follow rules and regulations out of a sense of duty, and fear of the consequences of disobedience, hoping for salvation in the future. Christians follow rules and regulations out of a sense of love and gratitude for a salvation *already received* in the present. A vast difference!

God's search for man

The story of religious movements is the story of man's search for God. 'They seek him here, they seek him there, those humans seek him everywhere.' People have looked for God in ritual and ceremony, in mystical experiences, in abstinence, in holy places, in religious belief and fervent devotion. They have searched in ancient faiths and in modern cults; in eastern magic and western materialism; in profound thought and orgies of emotion. The search has been unsuccessful. As unsuccessful as an ant trying to find the planet Jupiter! Man is simply not capable of this feat. Which is why Christianity is the story of the God who searches for man. It is the story of the God who wants to be known, and so introduces himself to us in the person of Jesus. In Christianity, unlike other religions, *God* has taken the initiative; he wants to be found. The details of his whereabouts are found in the Bible and the information is available to everyone. This God is not playing hard to get!

Real assurance

The Christian faith offers a sense of security. Ask a Christian if he is going to be with God for ever and he will answer 'yes'. Followers of other faiths will invariably say 'possibly' or 'perhaps'. It all depends on whether or not they can keep up their efforts and have more on the positive side than the negative side when they die. Because salvation is gained by earning merit you can never tell when you have earned enough, so you can never be sure that you are going to make it!

It's such a relief to know that God has done all that is necessary for our salvation – our only response is faith. Once we have made this commitment, he takes the waiting out of wanting. You want a certain hope for the future now, without waiting until you are dead to find out for sure whether or not you have made the grade? God offers this certainty *now* to those who receive his son.

Moral power

Other religions may offer us a discussion about water but Christianity offers a life-jacket! In other words, practical help when we are out of our depth. Christianity offers not just a code for life, but a power for living. When we become Christians, God's power comes into us and gives us strength to overcome all kinds of things in our lives we know are wrong. Power to defeat bad habits, alter our thinking, love the unlovely . . . a special offer of 'power for good' available only with this product.

And the story of the uniqueness of the Christian faith does not end there. We could talk about the way it is less culturally bound than other faiths, with Christians in every racial grouping. About how it cuts across barriers of age, sex, culture, continent and colour. About its unparalleled record of social concern and care for the underprivileged. About its survival under intense persecution.

We can only conclude that Christianity claims to be unique and, under scrutiny, shows itself to be unique. We are faced with a choice – is it right or wrong? The following chapters may help us decide.

4
What's so great about Jesus?

In 1970 the Beatles said that they had become more popular than Jesus. But the seventies saw the greatest modern explosion of interest in Jesus Christ; a positive glut of films, plays and books about this amazing character. Interest in Jesus continued to grow on into the eighties. By the end of 1986 the film *Jesus* had been translated into over eighty different languages and had been seen by more people than any other film ever produced! All this media attention has highlighted what ordinary people have thought for centuries: 'This Jesus character was something special'.

But what was he really like? Among the wilder suggestions have been that he was a gay hippy, or an alien from outer space, or a time traveller who turns up at various points in history whenever the world needs a little extra help. More seriously he has been portrayed as a political revolutionary, a great moral teacher, an eastern mystic and a misunderstood miracle-worker. Christians claim that he is not just a wonderful human being but also God; that he isn't dead now, although he was for a few days; and that he is very interested in making contact with every person on the planet. Let's try to put aside what we think we know about Jesus and examine the facts.

Did Jesus really exist?

There are still a few people who believe that Jesus was just a figment of someone's imagination. If this was so, it's strange that no one pointed out the fictitious nature of the Gospels when they were first circulated. For one thing, who were the brilliant minds who wove all that deep moral teaching into a sort of first-century novel? For another, all the manuscript evidence (see next chapter) points to reporters at work rather than novelists.

Besides this, how can we explain the impact on our world of Jesus Christ if he never existed? Many of the people who wrote the New Testament died because they wouldn't deny their faith in Jesus. But why die for a lie? Why not just say, 'Sorry chaps, big mistake, we made the whole thing up'?

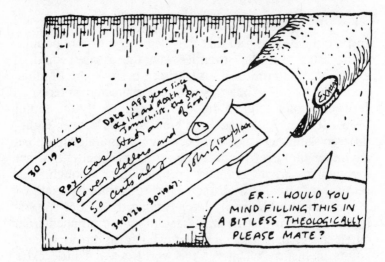

Whenever you date a letter or write a cheque you confirm the existence of Jesus. January 1st, 1988. 1,988 years since what? Since England won the Eurovision Song Contest? The invention of the wheel? Of course not. All of our history is divided between BC and AD – before Christ lived or after his birth. Fairy stories just couldn't exert this kind of lasting, global influence on our calendar.

Even if we dismiss the Bible's evidence for the existence of Jesus, we can still discover his presence in other early writings. In about AD 52, a man called Thalles wrote an account of the history of the mediterranean world. In it he mentioned Jesus being crucified, and tried to provide an explanation for the darkness which occurred at the same time (see Luke 23, verses 44 and 45). Pliny, a governor in a Roman province, wrote to the emperor about AD 112 and mentioned Jesus and his followers – he wanted advice about how to cope with them. Tacitus, a Roman historian writing in about AD 115, wrote of 'those who are commonly called Christians', and said that 'Christus, from whom their name is derived, was executed at the hands of the procurator Pontius Pilate in the reign of Tiberius'. (Tacitus, *Annals*, XV. 44.2–8.)

Probably the clearest report of first-century Christianity comes from Josephus, a Jewish general, living in exile in Rome. He writes towards the end of the first century, trying to describe the history of the Jews. In one part of this history he describes Jesus in some detail:

'Now, there was about this time Jesus, a wise man, if it be lawful to call him a man, for he was a doer of wonderful works, a teacher of such men as received the truth with pleasure. He drew over to him both many of the Jews and many of the Gentiles. He was the Christ. And when Pilate had condemned him to the cross, those that loved him at the first did not forsake him; for he appeared to them alive again at the third day; as the divine prophet had foretold these and ten thousand other wonderful things concerning him. And the tribe of Christians, so named from him, are not extinct at this day.' (*Antiquities of the Jews*, XVIII, 33.)

Not one of these men had Christian sympathies. Jesus was a problem they could have lived without, but they couldn't ignore him because they were historians and he was a fact of history. He was a flesh and blood first-century man. Just as real as Nelson, Napoleon or Winston Churchill!

Who was he?

That he actually lived is clear, but what kind of person was he? All the different suggestions that have been made boil down to four basic options.

A good man

This is way out in front as the clear favourite. A quick survey of the people in your place of work will reveal what a popular view this is. And it's not difficult to see why. The Gospels show him as kind and considerate, keen to help people, especially the underprivileged. A man who wanted to right wrongs and see justice done; to bring peace and joy to replace unrest and sadness.

So far so good. But it's only half the story. Alongside all this niceness he kept on saying and doing things which good men couldn't or wouldn't say or do! Eyewitnesses saw him walk on water and heal hundreds of people. They saw him calm a storm and raise people from the dead. He said the kind of things which even the most conceited bighead would never dare say. Things like, 'If you believe in me you will live for ever', and 'I am the only way to get to God'. He claimed to be able to forgive sins and talk directly to God – who he called his father. He said he had been given all the power in the universe and that he had always been in existence! He challenged an angry crowd to find a single sin in his life (and they couldn't!) and he was happy to let people worship him.

Now think of some of the really good people you know or have heard about. It's hard to imagine Mother Teresa claiming to have always been in existence, or Bob Geldof offering to forgive your sins! There have been hundreds of good people over the years, yet not a single one of them (precisely because they were good) would have dreamed of saying the things Jesus did. And the same is true of all the religious teachers in history. Confucius, Buddha, Socrates, Muhammad . . . none of them ever claimed anything like this. Good men don't say this kind of thing. And the people who met Jesus knew this. In the New Testament we meet those who loved him and those who hated him; very few sitting on the fence. This was because what he said was so shocking. As shocking as the Pope appearing on television and claiming to be God. No, the 'good man' option simply doesn't fit the facts.

A mad man

I have met people who made claims like those Jesus made. Some have claimed to be God himself, some just of being his special messenger, and others claiming supernatural powers. All of these people were in mental institutions! Perhaps Jesus ought to be included with them, as just another well-meaning but deluded lunatic. Was he sincere but unbalanced? Let's look at the evidence.

First *his character*: he was patient with his followers, kind to children, always appearing in control of himself and the situation, compassionate, and always ready to respond to cries for help. Second *his teaching:* clear cohesive statements about life and death issues, well-illustrated guidelines for human behaviour, and a depth and perception in his statements about God which are simply light years ahead of anything else in religious literature. Third, *his relationships:* a loyal son, a faithful friend and a fearless leader. Fourth, *his abilities:* superb in public debate, demolishing his opponents' arguments with rapier-like thrusts of logic; skill at relating to people in any strata of society, and awareness of greatness without a trace of pomposity.

If all this describes madness may I be struck down with it immediately! In fact the personality of Jesus and the power of his message point to a profound sanity.

A bad man

Which brings us to option three. What if Jesus was just a con-man? A liar who deceived people into believing his message? This supposes that people in the first century were idiots; some would have been fooled of course, but sooner or later he would have been rumbled. Yet throughout his entire life no one was ever able to expose him as a fraud or even discover inconsistencies between what he said and the way he lived. All we know about his life – his moral purity, his deep concerns, his teaching – does not add up to a description of a manipulative schemer. To believe that Jesus was such a superb con-man that he could take on all these good qualities and keep them consistently, fool every close friend and then be willing to die to keep up the fraud, would stretch imagination to breaking point. There is not a single piece of evidence which shows him deceiving, manipulating or lying; and he was poor throughout his life and penniless at his death.

Before we move on to option four, let's look at the implications of our discussion so far. Each of the first three options could be true about part of the life of Jesus. For instance, if we had a record only of his kind actions, the 'good man' option would fit the facts perfectly; if we only had his wild claims to be God, no one would argue with the 'mad man' tag; and, if we only had his promises without any fulfilment, 'bad man' would be written against his name without hesitation. But we don't! We have lots of information about Jesus and we must examine all of it.

A blind man was asked to describe an elephant after only feeling its tail. 'An elephant is like a rope' he said confidently. But an examination of all the data (the trunk, head, shoulders, etc.) would show that the man was wrong – an elephant is nothing like a rope. Far too many descriptions of Jesus are pretty ropey! They don't do justice to all the evidence at our disposal.

A God-man

This option affirms that Jesus was a very special human being and also that he was God. Completely human and completely divine. God and man in the same person. This is a staggering statement; but however remarkable it appears, it fits the facts we have better than anything else.

Hardly anyone would dispute the first part of this option – Jesus was very special. Thousands of thinking people have written or spoken about the impact of Jesus on our world. Statesmen, philosphers, scientists, poets and leaders in every sphere of society. Christians and non-Christians, those writing in history and those speaking today, academics from every discipline – all have acknowledged the massive impact this first-century Jew has had on our planet. This anonymous statement sums it up well:

'He was born in an obscure village, the child of a peasant woman. He grew up in yet another village, where he worked in a carpenter's shop till he was thirty. Then for three years he was an itinerant preacher.

He never wrote a book. He never held an office. He never had a family or owned a house. He didn't go to college. He never visited a big city. He never travelled more than 200 miles from the place where he was born. He did none of the things one usually associates with greatness. He had no credentials but himself.

He was only thirty-three when the tide of public opinion turned against him. His friends ran away. He was nailed to a cross between two thieves. While he was dying, his executioners gambled for his clothing, the only property he had on earth.

Nineteen centuries have come and gone and today he is the central figure of the human race. All the armies that ever marched, all the navies that ever sailed, all the parliaments that ever sat, all the kings that ever reigned, put together, have not affected the life of man on this earth as much as that one solitary life!'

No question about it, this Jesus was unique.

But is he God? Well, he certainly claimed to be. He took the special Hebrew name for God and used it of himself. He didn't stop people worshipping him; he forgave sins, raised the dead and said that to receive him was to receive God! Peter thought that he was God ('you are the Christ, the son of the living God') and so did Thomas ('my Lord and my God').[5] Paul, John, Stephen and John the Baptist made clear statements about his divinity.

His enemies were in no doubt either. The reason they

wanted to get rid of him was because he claimed he was equal to God, ' . . . because you, a mere man, claim to be God'.[6] The early Christians were not in any doubt either. Even the leader of the whole Roman empire was made aware of it in a letter from one of his administrators, Pliny. Writing to him about Christians, he says, 'They were in the habit of meeting on a fixed day before it was light, when they sang in alternate verse a hymn to Christ as a God.' (Pliny to Trajan, *Epp*. X. 96.) The early church thought that Jesus was God, and Christians continue to believe it today. Even a battle-hardened general like Napoleon cannot escape this conclusion, 'I think I understand something of human nature, and I tell you none else is like him; Jesus Christ was more than man.' There follows a description of Jesus' incredible authority, and then Napoleon's conclusion: 'This it is which proves to me quite convincingly the divinity of Jesus Christ.' (From a conversation quoted by HP Lydon in *The Divinity of our Lord and Saviour, Jesus Christ*; Rivingtons.)

So there is a great deal of testimony that points to Jesus being God and man. Now we are not saying that this is an easy option; just that it makes the most sense of all the data available. It is horrendously difficult to imagine God and man in the same person, but it would be quite wrong to reject this option simply because it blows our mind. Scientists tell us that two theories are needed to explain how light works – one theory says that light is made up of particles, the other that it consists of waves. Neither theory on its own is enough to explain what light is; both are needed. Yet science has still not discovered how the two things work together. It defies imagination. However, scientists have accepted it because it's the best explanation of the facts we have. Similarly, we cannot explain how God and man could both be present in the person of Jesus. However, a thorough, open appraisal of everything Jesus said and did leads to this conclusion. No other theory comes anywhere close to accounting for all the data we have available on Jesus of Nazareth.

But did he rise from the dead?

Of course, if he was God this wouldn't be a problem. But let's examine the Bible's account of what happened. Jesus was betrayed by a close associate, tried by the Jews, handed over to the Romans and executed by crucifixion. After his death he was placed in a tomb provided by a wealthy supporter. On Sunday morning some women came to visit his grave only to discover that he was not dead any more, but alive. Usually dead men don't come back to life, so some people have a hard time with the simple statement in the Gospels, 'He is risen'. A number of alternative possibilities have been suggested.

Jesus never really died

He revived in the tomb and then went to the disciples to give them his final instructions. This theory asks us to believe that a man who had been brutally beaten, strung up on a cross for six hours with nails in his hands and feet and a spear rammed into his side is still alive. Then, after at least thirty-six hours in a cold tomb, he can unwrap himself from yards of cloth soaked in thirty-four kilogrammes of spice, push away a stone so huge that three women could not budge it, fight his way past the guard, walk miles on nail-damaged feet and then appear to his disciples as a picture of health, the conqueror of death! Enough said. You would need more gullibility than King Canute to believe this.

Somebody moved the body

But who? Not the Jewish or Roman authorities, that's for sure. In less than six weeks all of Jerusalem was buzzing with rumours about Jesus being alive. Within three months the rumours had become a tidal wave of popular opinion resulting in acute embarrassment for the authorities. Religious values were being challenged and revolution was in the air; and all on the basis of Jesus being alive. All this could have been stopped in its tracks if the body had been produced. Why wasn't it? Because obviously the authorities did not have it. And it's hard to imagine the followers of Jesus taking it. The chances of this timorous crowd coming up with such an idea, overpowering the guards and so brilliantly hiding the body that it was never discovered, are extremely remote. Especially as you would have to come up with an explanation about why they went on to risk death on the basis of a lie. It's hard to believe they could spend the rest of their lives living as if Jesus were alive when they knew his body was actually rotting away in some unmarked Galilean grave. No, this explanation causes more problems than it solves.

The disciples hallucinated
People do have hallucinations: they see or hear things which are not really there. But what we have in the evidence before us seems to exclude this possibility. Jesus appeared on a dozen occasions to individuals and to groups of his followers, in very different locations. Once he appeared to a crowd of over five hundred people. And these were not fleeting glimpses – here one minute, gone the next. They were often prolonged interviews. Hallucinations are usually a result of some kind of wish-fulfilment; but the disciples themselves took some convincing! The resurrection was a complete surprise to them.

In addition to these three main explanations other, more fanciful, options have been suggested. (For instance, robbers stole the body, the women went to the wrong tomb, they crucified the wrong man.) All of them are selective in their use of the facts and a cursory glance reveals what empty explanations they are, particularly in the light of what went on soon after Jesus had died, and has continued right up to the present day.

Look what happened to the disciples! They were transformed from a terrified rabble into a group who fearlessly proclaimed their message. They can heal the sick, beat the Jewish academics in a debate and go gladly to cruel deaths for their beliefs. What on earth brought about such an amazing change?

Look what happened to the church! It began just after the death of Jesus. Its impact was incredible. First three thousand people, then five thousand, then a large number of Jewish priests were won over to become followers of Jesus. The message spread like wildfire in the ancient world. Down the centuries the church has been persecuted and ridiculed; yet it still continues to go from strength to strength. What event could have triggered off the start of this enduring institution?

Look what happened to the Sabbath! It got changed to Sunday! Remember, most of the disciples were Jews brought up to observe the Sabbath (Saturday). It was one of the most fervently held tenets of Judaism; a centuries-old custom which was absolutely binding on every Jew. What happened to cause this major break with tradition?

All these things point to some stupendous event. If not the resurrection, what? No other satisfactory explanation has been put forward. The evidence in favour of it is convincing. No less a person than Lord Darling, a former Lord Chief Justice of England, says of the resurrection, 'In its favour as a living truth there exists such overwhelming evidence, positive and negative, factual and circumstantial, that no intelligent jury in the world could fail to bring in a verdict that the resurrection story is true.'

The issue of the resurrection of Jesus is at the heart of the Christian faith. If you could produce an alternative theory which more completely explained all the evidence, I would have to be honest enough to abandon my Christianity. On the other hand, if you can't, you would have to be honest enough to follow the evidence to its logical conclusion – the resurrection of Jesus really happened!

5
The Bible – can we trust it?

No one in their right mind could ever doubt that the Bible is a remarkable book. It has been the number one best seller for decades. Each year people buy hundreds of millions. In addition, one Bible distribution group (the Gideons) claims to give away one million copies every twenty-seven days. Parts of it are available in nearly two thousand languages and each year sees translations into yet more languages.

And all this despite the fact that the Bible is no light-weight paperback novel. Not exactly easy reading! Actually, the Bible is not a single book but a collection of sixty-six books, written by about forty authors, using over three-quarters of a million words, over a period spanning more than a thousand years. And there is an amazing harmony from beginning to end.

It has been the most discussed, debated and quoted book in history. Abraham Lincoln ('I believe the Bible is the best gift God has given to man') and hundreds of statesmen since have paid tribute to its value. Charles Dickens ('the New Testament is the very best book that ever was or ever will be known in the world') and countless authors since have drawn their inspiration from its pages. Millions of ordinary men and women from every background and occupation have found strength and guidance in its teaching. Yes, the Bible is certainly a remarkable book.

But no thinking person will be content to leave it at that. 'Is the Bible true?' is the crucial question. After all, millions of newspapers are sold every day. Does the vast number of them guarantee that they are telling the truth? Hardly! So the sheer number of Bibles doesn't guarantee the truthfulness of what it says. What about all the contradictions and those unbelievable miracle stories? Perhaps the writers just made up the whole thing. Did the people in the Bible stories really exist? Is there any evidence to support what the Bible says? Is it really any help to sophisticated, scientific men and women at the end of the twentieth century? Let's examine the facts about this book.

Miracles

There are certainly a lot of miraculous events recorded in the Bible. The Israelites crossing the Red Sea without getting their feet wet. Five thousand people enjoying a free lunch, and all from a few loaves of bread and a couple of fish. A man who had been dead for four days being brought back to life; and lots more. We can't just ignore the miracles in the Bible; they are an essential part of the book. Take them away and there is no message left, because at the very heart of Christianity we find the miracle of God becoming a man in Jesus and the miracle of Jesus being raised from the dead. Without these miracles the Christian faith falls flat on its face; it becomes a set of pious platitudes supported by some common-sense advice. We would be left with a much briefer Bible but a message that had ceased to be Christianity!

We can't explain the miracles away either. Some people try of course, often by assuming that in Bible times people were ignorant and superstitious, simple and primitive. This view disregards the evidence of history which reveals a much less naïve view of the miraculous than we may have expected. People then may have been a little gullible and superstitious – but they weren't stupid! They knew just as well as we do that virgins don't give birth to babies, dead men stay dead and that walking on water is not a normal human activity. The eyewitnesses of these incidents couldn't explain what had happened, but neither could they ignore the evidence of their senses.

And they didn't give in easily. Paul wouldn't believe a word of it until he experienced a miracle himself on the way to Damascus. Mary gave the angel a hard time before feeling confident about the miracle she was to take part in – the virgin birth. And of course there's Thomas the cynic who said he wasn't going to fall for any of that resurrection stuff until he had some proof. Real tangible proof.

All this may be true, but aren't miracles impossible because they break the laws of nature? Well, the laws of nature are generalizations about what usually happens. They don't explain why it happens or why it should *always* happen. Scientific laws cannot, by definition, exclude the possibility of miracles. Of course, by their very nature miracles are not common, but that doesn't mean they never happen. Remarkably improbable things *do* happen. The odds against being dealt a perfect hand in bridge are 635,013,559, 600 to one – but it has happened! The probability of finding a church minister wearing his pyjamas during morning worship must be astronomically low. But it did happen one Easter Sunday at a Baptist Church in Luton, England. And there are dozens of witnesses who could testify (with some amusement) that this event occurred. Some of the Bible miracles may seem very unlikely but it doesn't mean that they didn't happen.

Funnily enough, this business of the miraculous has become less of a problem to most people in the last quarter of the twentieth century. There has been an explosion of interest in the occult and paranormal. Have real UFO's been sighted? Does faith-healing work? Can we see into the future? People have become much more open to the fact that there are forces at work over which we have little control. And, of course, Christians claim that miracles occur today. I know literally dozens of them who have an event in their lives they simply cannot explain in any way other than by using the word 'miracle'. They are not emotional, gullible people either, and we have to take their evidence seriously.

If we have decided in advance that miracles can't occur, no amount of evidence would convince us otherwise. But for the genuine, honest enquirer, the miracles of the Bible need not be a barrier to discovering the message at its heart.

Contradictions?

Sooner or later, there is a discussion at work or college about the Bible. Nearly always someone comments on all the contradictions in it. Sometimes it's not a question – 'How can you believe a book so full of contradictions?' – but a confident statement: 'The Bible is full of contradictions'. Now I have a suspicion that the vast majority of people who say that have never read the Bible thoroughly. A Bible is often treated like a dictionary – most homes have one, but hardly anyone ever uses it. We ask a friend how to spell a word rather than look it up. It's quicker, but much less reliable. Lots of people get their knowledge of the Bible this way – second-hand. Many of those who make dogmatic statements about the inconsistencies in the Bible are simply talking through their hats! They are repeating well-worn clichés handed on to them by someone else. When asked to produce even *one* of these supposed contradictions they are usually at a complete loss.

Here is another dogmatic statement, and I would like to produce some evidence to support it: 'The Bible is *not* full of contradictions.' I have read the Bible from start to finish; some parts of it many times. I have discovered quite a few things which seemed to contradict each other. They were all relatively incidental things, certainly not anything which remotely affected the message of the book. What's more, the greater my understanding of the ancient languages and Jewish culture, and the more closely I study the actual texts, I discover that I can find a perfectly reasonable explanation for some of the apparent inconsistencies.

And I'm not the only one. Thousands of serious scholars have given much of their lives to in-depth study of the Bible and have emerged with an even greater confidence in its reliability. One of these academics, Dr Gleason Archer (Professor of Semitic studies at Trinity Evangelical Divinity School, Illinios), has put together a book which deals with almost all these alleged inconsistencies. In the preface to the book he is able to write:

'As I have dealt with one apparent discrepancy after another and have studied the alleged contradictions between the biblical record and the evidence of linguistics, archaeology, or science, my confidence in the trustworthiness of scripture has been repeatedly verified and strengthened by the discovery that almost every problem in scripture that had ever been discovered by man, from ancient times until now, has been dealt with in a completely satisfactory manner by the biblical text itself – or else by objective archaeological information.' (Gleason Archer, *Encyclopedia of Bible Difficulties*; Zondervan.)

Don't take Dr Archer's word on this, or mine; find out for yourself. If you read the Bible with an open mind I think you're going to come to the same conclusion.

A message from God to be trusted?

The Bible claims to be God's message to the world. I want to give five reasons why I think that this is a genuine claim; five pieces of evidence which make me confident that it is absolutely trustworthy and permanently relevant.

Manuscripts

A large part of the Bible deals with eyewitness accounts; first-hand information. And it was passed on with meticulous care. Even today, Jews repeat their traditional teaching and stories in just the same form as they did centuries ago. Besides, all the New Testament books were written down only forty years after Jesus died. Just think how hard it would be to describe the years after the Second World War as ' . . . petrol was plentiful, no rationing, hardly any bomb damage in London and plenty of money for everyone.' There are thousands of people alive today who would say you were lying. They were there! So, when the New Testament books were first circulating, there would have been uproar if the facts were inaccurate or simply made up.

When the first manuscripts were copied they weren't done in some cavalier, haphazard fashion. The Jewish copyists took their work seriously: the discovery of even the smallest error could lead to the whole manuscript being destroyed and work beginning all over again. There are thousands of these copies available to study, and they give us a remarkably accurate picture of the original documents. This is what makes the Bible unique. There are simply no other writings from this period with anything like the support the Bible has. Everyone believes that Julius Caesar came to Britain in 55 BC. But we only have nine or ten manuscripts to support this, and the earliest was written 900 years after the event! In contrast, we have over two thousand manuscripts of the Gospels, some of which were written only two hundred years after the event. As time goes by, earlier manuscripts come to light which confirm the accuracy of the later copies. (The oldest fragment of a manuscript we have discovered so far can be seen in the

John Ryland's Library, Manchester, England. It is dated 130 AD – only a few decades after the original was written!) John Robinson, a Cambridge professor, is so impressed by the manuscript evidence that he says,

'The wealth of manuscripts, and above all the narrow interval of time between the writing and the earliest extant copies, make it by far the best attested text of any ancient writing in the world.' (John Robinson, *Can we trust the New Testament*? Mowbrays.)

So what we have in the Bible is a very well documented, carefully compiled piece of literature; an authentic record of events, preserved over the centuries with unequalled accuracy. It cannot be dismissed lightly.

Archaeology
Digging around in ancient ruins is not everyone's idea of a good time, but this painstaking and detailed work has produced some compelling evidence to support the accuracy of many Bible passages. Time after time those who question the integrity of the Bible have to retreat in the face of clear archaeological evidence. William Ramsey went to the Middle East expecting to discover archaeological evidence which would confirm the inaccuracies of the Bible. He found precisely the opposite! Every piece of evidence he uncovered showed how reliable the biblical record was. Others have discovered this since. Donald Wiseman, Professor of Assyriology at London University, writes, 'No fact of archaeology so far discovered contradicts the biblical record.' (D Wiseman, *Digging for Truth*, Viewpoint no 31; Inter School Christian Fellowship.) Dr J O Kinnaman writes,

'Of the hundreds of thousands of artefacts found by the archaeologists, not one has ever been discovered that contradicts or denies one word, phrase, clause or sentence of the Bible.' (*The Encyclopaedia of 7700 Illustrations*; Assurance.)

We have archaeological evidence from as long ago as two thousand BC, which confirms many of the details given in the Bible – facts about the city Abraham came from; the unearthing of some of Solomon's military installations; inscriptions from the time of Moses; and remarkable confirmation that the Jews really did go into exile in the sixth century BC. Turning to the New Testament, scholars had dismissed, for example, John's description of the Pool of Bethesda in chapter five of his Gospel as 'poetic licence'. But archaeologists have now excavated the whole site and discovered all five porches and an inscription saying that the water has healing properties! Luke has been confirmed as a reliable historian and Paul as an accurate author.

All this should help us get away from the idea that the Bible is a collection of fairy tales, a sort of spiritual *Aesop's Fables*. It isn't. It is a message with its roots in history and its basis in fact.

Prophecy
Another thing that makes the Bible such an amazing book is the way it predicts events in the future, which then happen. I don't mean the sort of thing you can read in your average horoscope – 'Today you will meet a handsome stranger. Tomorrow it will be dry if it's not raining.' I mean specific predictions which are unmistakably fulfilled. There are hundreds of them in the Bible. For example, Ezekiel predicted in the sixth century before Christ that Tyre (a major city and thriving industrial centre) would be defeated and utterly destroyed. Nebuchadnezzar, and then Alexander the Great, brought about the fulfilment of this prophecy. It even says in Ezekiel chapter 26 verse 14, 'I will leave only a bare rock where fishermen can dry their nets.' Sure enough, after Tyre was taken over by the Arabs in 1291 AD, it became a poor fishing village. Among many other fulfilled predictions, Amos foretold the downfall of Israel, Jeremiah the capture of Jerusalem, Isaiah the return from exile and Jesus the destruction of Jerusalem.

Jesus' own coming to earth was predicted in a precise

way. He was to be born in Bethlehem (Micah 5:2). He would enter Jerusalem on a donkey (Zechariah 9:9), be rejected and killed (Isaiah 53:3–5), while men gambled for his clothes (Psalm 22:18). All these predictions were made over four hundred years before Jesus came. Each one happened. In fact, not a single prediction in the Bible can be shown to be false – a remarkable record.

Survival under attack
The Bible has had its enemies. Despite this it has resisted all their attacks and its influence continues to grow. This is even more remarkable when you consider the nature of the opposition.

There has been opposition from philosophers. Some have relegated the Bible to the level of ancient superstition, a set of ideas appropriate to the dawn of civilization but irrelevant to our advancing culture. Voltaire, an eighteenth-century French philosopher, predicted that the Bible's days were numbered and that an enlightened world would soon discard it. More advanced philosophies would take over. But over two hundred years after his death the Bible is more widely read than ever before. The ironic thing is, Voltaire's old house in France is now used as a storage and distribution centre for a Bible society! (And, by the way, who reads Voltaire today?)

There has been opposition from governments. Over the last two thousand years of Christianity, the Bible has, from time to time, been outlawed. During the French Revolution it was seen as an instrument of aristocratic oppression, and owning or reading one was officially discouraged. Rousseau's *Social Contract* was seen as a much more significant piece of litera-ture for the salvation of France. In the twentieth century we have seen the rise of atheistic communism, particularly in Russia and China. Millions of people live under govern-ments which actively discourage the ownership and reading of the Bible. Printing presses are destroyed and the printers put in prison. If spoken of at all, it is dismissed as capitalist propaganda unworthy of consideration in the new world of the revolution. But, after more than sixty years of attack, there is still a great demand for Bibles behind the iron curtain. More and more Soviet young people want to read it for themselves and many Christian groups are crying out to the West for more copies of the Bible to meet growing demand. Similar things are happening in China. What is certain is that years of government pressure have not dented the Bible's defences; if anything its popularity grows.

There has been opposition from the church! Well, sections of it anyway. Liberal theologians have tried to discredit the accuracy of the biblical record; labelling the Gospels, for example, as clever stories which came largely from the imagination of the writers. However, where we *can* check the details of the stories with outside sources, the Bible proves accurate. For example, Josephus, a Jewish historian, confirms the ministry of John the Baptist, the death of Herod Agrippa and Pilate's role in the death of Jesus. All these events were historical facts, known and recorded because they happened. What's more, the 'clever stories' theory is also rejected by many experts in the field of literature. C S Lewis, who lectured in English Literature for almost forty years at both Oxford and Cambridge Universities, said that after examining many different kinds of literature he was convinced that there are only two possible views of the Gospels. Either they are reports of actual events or someone came up with the modern novel-writing technique over fifteen hundred years before anyone else! He found the second view incredible.

It seems that the evidence from literature studies and from historical sources confirms that the statements in the Bible are reliable accounts of real events.

Opposition to the Bible is likely to continue. Some new theory will question its accuracy, some public figure will pour scorn on it and any day now another TV documentary will attempt to discredit it with some half-baked theory cloaked in a veneer of academic respectability. If the Bible can take the worst things the last two thousand years has thrown at it, and still be flourishing, it seems unlikely to be in danger from any twentieth-century critic. About as much danger as a tank being damaged by a peashooter!

It works!

This is the crunch. The other four things all point to the reliability of the Bible but this section brings the issue right down to earth. The Bible makes sense of the world, provides an explanation for what's gone wrong and gives a blueprint for change. And this blueprint works. Millions of people (and I'm not exaggerating) have read the Bible and found that it was like looking into a mirror. Everything it said about human nature was true about them. This discovery is very depressing because the Bible has no qualms about describing the mess we are in: greed, pride, envy, lust and selfishness of every kind. No sugary coating on this bitter pill! What makes it even harder to swallow is that no one escapes judgment; no one at all. It's not all bad news though. The Bible does go on to describe the antidote to all this – a clean sheet, wrong things forgiven and a new power for living. I have experienced this myself and have found the message of the Bible to be true.

Actually, none of this will come as a surprise to anyone who accepts what the Bible says about itself. It claims to be a message from God to every human being – no wonder what it says is true and really works in changing people's lives. You can always test this claim for yourself. Get a modern translation of the Bible and turn to the Gospel of John. Read it carefully and with an open mind. Persevere to the end of the Gospel and keep asking yourself, 'What response do I need to make if this is true?' Ask a Christian you know to explain any bits you can't understand. If you don't know any Christians, make an appointment to see your local pastor, minister or vicar – he won't bite your head off! You will discover what a powerful book the Bible is.

6
Science and faith – a fatal encounter?

Science rules OK! That could easily be the most accurate slogan for the last part of the twentieth century. Science, and its offspring, technology (the practical application of science), have come to dominate our world. In the home – videos, microwaves, computers and dishwashers. In the hospital – new drugs, micro-surgery, computerized diagnostic apparatus and a bewildering array of monitoring devices. Cars that talk ('I need oil!') built by robots that don't. TV sets that will pay your gas bill and buy airline tickets to America at the touch of a button. Science fiction is rapidly becoming science fact.

As science answers more and more questions, it is inevitable that some people will begin to ask whether science can answer the ultimate questions of life. After all, science has progressed amazingly in finding out about human beings, the beginnings of life on our planet and the origins of the universe – so is it well on the way to providing an answer to *all* our questions? Is Christianity bound for the scrap heap of history as a belief that was all right for our more superstitious ancestors, but is no use to modern scientific man? If this is so let's be honest enough to leave it behind and move on to scientific maturity. But has science really sounded the death-knell for Christianity?

We are often told that science and faith are in conflict – and not left in much doubt about which one is wrong! 'People *used* to believe that, but science has shown it not to be true.' End of contest. A knock-out victory for science over faith in the first round. But is this simplistic view of the relationship between science and faith accurate? Let's look at the three main areas where the conflict is supposed to be most fierce.

Conflict in history?

'Christianity and science have always been in conflict', some people say. They remind us about Galileo getting into trouble with the church authorities for saying that the earth revolved around the sun. The church was apparently very annoyed because they saw the earth as the centre of everything and wanted to believe all the other planets and stars revolved around it. Then they point to the famous debate in 1860 between T H Huxley and Bishop Wilberforce in which the Bishop ridiculed the scientific view of evolution by asking Huxley whether he was related to a monkey through his grandmother or his grandfather! This exchange produced more heat than light and resulted in the scientific community accusing the church of being completely closed to reasonable discussion. And what about John Lightfoot in the seventeenth century? He used the Bible to calculate that the world came into existence on the 18th of October and that man was made at nine in the morning on October 23rd, 4004 BC!

Whenever the subject of science or faith crops up – in

TV documentaries, text books, discussion with science students – these illustrations are trotted out to 'prove' that conflict exists. But if this conflict is as obvious as some people say it is, why aren't there dozens and dozens of examples to demonstrate it? After all, modern scientific enquiry has been around for over four hundred years, which is enough time to gather a few more examples! There are, of course, other examples of conflict between scientific and religious establishments – but they are surprisingly rare. There is simply no compelling evidence that Christianity has ever 'had it in for' science.

Even these three supposedly cast-iron illustrations are open to debate. Perhaps the Wilberforce–Huxley conflict tells us as much about a scientific community which thought itself above contradiction as it does about an opinionated bishop with a sense of humour! Not every theologian and church leader agreed with Lightfoot's dates for the creation of the world. In fact, he had as much opposition from inside the church as outside.

More serious still, there doesn't seem to be any real evidence that the Galileo story happened as it is so often related. An examination of the facts is difficult because of incomplete documentation, but such evidence as there is shows substantial differences from the popular story. The idea that the earth was not the centre of the planetary system was not new. Copernicus (a priest as well as a scientist) had said the same thing a hundred years earlier. Kepler, over thirty years before Galileo's 'trial', had openly declared that the earth went round the sun. He received support and protection from the Catholic Church despite the fact that he was a Lutheran! Galileo's view was not news to his questioners. The church was willing to adjust to Galileo's opinion if he could produce evidence for his particular theory about why the earth went round the sun; no compelling evidence was forthcoming. His 'sentence' was a token gesture expressing the church's disagreement; he was not stopped from continuing his scientific investigation. In fact he went on to make his most significant contribution to science after the 'trial', in the field of dynamics. Arthur Koestler (certainly not a supporter of Christianity!) in his examination of this issue says that it is quite wrong to see the incident as a 'showdown between "blind faith" and "enlightened reason".' (Arthur Koestler, *The Sleep Walkers*; Pelican.)

All in all, none of these three incidents gives us good evidence of a continuing conflict in history. In fact, the examples of conflict seem to me to be the exception rather than the rule. Certainly we would expect this to be so when we realize that the rise of modern science can be linked to biblical Christianity. Many of the first scientists were Christians (among them Francis Bacon, Isaac Newton, Robert Boyle) as the Christian world view encouraged careful investigation of the universe God had made. It was in this atmosphere that modern scientific enquiry was born. R E D Clark (a leading scientist in Cambridge) can state categorically, 'There is little doubt that the scientific movement of the seventeenth century owed its origin to the Christian faith.' (R E D Clark, *Christian Belief and Science;* EUP.) Far from being an enemy, science was in fact a product of thoughtful Christianity. From the birth of science to the present day there is no cohesive evidence to demonstrate that Christian faith and scientific enquiry are opposed.

Conflict in principle?

Aren't science and Christianity poles apart in their basic stance? Doesn't one deal in facts and the other in faith? Doesn't one give proof and the other ask for belief? Hasn't science done away with the need for faith? Let's examine what science actually is.

Science makes observations, carries out experiments, formulates hypotheses, tests them, defines them and then produces a theory which it believes best explains the facts. It is trying to get at the truth about how our world works. But it is only one aspect of the truth. For example, you could say, as a scientist, that playing the violin was 'rubbing the entrails of a dead sheep with the hairs of a dead horse' – and you would be describing the facts accurately. But not all the facts. You would not be answering the question of why certain sounds are harmonious and others not, why the music is enjoyable or why the violinist is playing at all. Strictly speaking, science can only answer the 'how' questions not the 'why' questions.

This is an important fact to grasp. To the question 'why is the grass burning?' a scientist could answer by talking about the presence of oxygen, the combustible nature of grass, wind factors, and so on. But this is actually a description of *what* is occurring not an explanation of *why* it is occurring. The answer to the 'why' question could be a carelessly discarded cigarette, a farmer clearing his waste ground or a malicious prankster! It is precisely in the 'why' area that Christianity has so much to say. Science cannot help us with issues like right and wrong, beauty, peace, joy and love – they are simply outside its scope. These subjects do not yield their secrets to the laboratory or the study. God cannot be put under a microscope or the Christian faith examined in a test-tube. These things are beyond the realm of scientific enquiry.

So we have established that science and Christianity are different in that they answer different questions. But there is an important point of similarity. Both are based on faith! (Scientists call them presuppositions – but they can't be scientifically proved and so are really statements of faith.) Now this comes as quite a shock to a lot of people who think that science is all about facts. In reality, all of science is based on at least two statements of faith:

1. The universe is an orderly place. It works on a uniform, regular basis.
2. The information received by our senses and minds is an accurate picture of the universe.

Now it is absolutely impossible to 'prove' either of these statements scientifically. And yet, if you don't accept them there is no point bothering with scientific investigation. If, for example, the second statement wasn't true, science would be like trying to receive TV programmes on a set with no aerial. The screen would be blurred at best, blank at worst. If your senses only perceive the universe in this kind of way, science becomes a cosmic guessing game of little practical relevance. What we actually believe is that our scientific aerial is secure and that as we continue to tune our science in we get a clearer and clearer picture of what the universe is like. Neither of these two beliefs of science can, however, be proved, any more than 'there is a God' or 'Jesus died for me' can be proved scientifically.

Science and Christianity are both based on assumptions that cannot be proved. Perhaps this fact ought to make us a little more cautious about the dogmatic statements of some scientists and a little more open to examine the claims of Christianity.

One of the most convincing reasons for not seeing any real conflict in principle between science and Christianity is a practical one. So many scientists are Christians! Intelligent men and women in every field of scientific research see absolutely no conflict between what they believe as scientists and what they believe as Christians. For example:

'If I didn't believe that I had a God who was solid and dependable, a God who makes no mistakes, I couldn't continue what I'm doing. I think the hallmark of my existence is the integration of my surgical life with my Christian faith. (Dr C Everett Koop; United States Surgeon General.)

'I can claim that I have made several discoveries in my field, but none of them compares with the greatest discovery I have ever made. That happened in December 1958, when I discovered that Christ was indeed my Saviour, Lord and God – and not only my Saviour but the Saviour of the whole world.' (Dr Robert Selvendran; Biochemist. Both quotes from Barratt and Fisher, *Scientists Who Believe*; Moody Press.)

In addition to these two I have statements from a professor

of medical genetics, a physicist, a meteorologist, a mathematician, and about thirty other leading academics . . . all on my desk as I write this chapter.

These two sections have been an attempt to show that in history and in the principles they use, science and Christianity are not in conflict. The next section looks at the apparent conflict in more obvious practical areas.

Conflict in popular opinion?

Many people seem to feel that, given enough time, science will solve the world's problems. Cancer and heart disease will become a thing of the past; new strains of quick-growing crops will feed the hungry, and increased automation will give us extra hours of leisure and relaxation. Christianity, it is said, may give people a sense of well-being or personal fulfilment, but it is never going to solve our world's major dilemmas.

This is a terrible misconception. Science is *not* going to solve anything. Nuclear power can heat our homes or wipe every living thing off the face of the earth. Laser beams can cut metal or the human body. Space science could lead to a colony on the moon or a *Star Wars* blood bath in the sky! It's what we *do* with our scientific advances that counts. Despite the incredible advances in scientific knowledge in this century alone, we would be hard pressed to show that the world has become a better place. Global political instability, international terrorism and the threat of a nuclear holocaust make short work of that idea. In some ways advances in science are extremely dangerous and may be part of the problem, not part of the solution! If a child got hold of a bow and arrow it would be dangerous, but if it got hold of a bomb the consequences are unthinkable. The human race is playing with ever more lethal toys, yet hasn't grown up enough to avoid the consequences of using them.

Christianity says that scientific advances are important but they can't deal with the root cause of the problem – man himself. As long as greed, selfishness, hatred and prejudice are around, the world's problems cannot be solved by any new discovery, however wonderful it may be. Science does not have anything to say about solving these basic human failings. Christianity claims that only a completely new start with God solves these problems. Of course Christians don't claim to be perfect in these areas. It's just that now they have a new power inside them to fight against these things. They believe that only when these fundamental issues of human nature are dealt with will we have a hope of solving the world's problems.

Perhaps the greatest conflict between science and faith in the popular mind is seen in the media. Most of us do not read scientific journals, and wouldn't understand them if we did! We can watch TV programmes or read our newspapers and this is where most people get their scientific information from. Sadly, this information is sometimes inaccurate and often misleading. A scientific paper of any weight is hedged around with qualifications – 'given these conditions', 'other experiments pending', 'on the data available' – and is fairly tentative until much more evidence is examined. But this makes for boring television and dull articles in the press and so what we are presented with are certainties. 'Major breakthrough' and 'new discovery' are much more exciting than the 'may be', 'possibly' and 'perhaps' of true science. This leaves your average man in the pub with the impression that definite statements of provable fact are being made. In contrast, the Christian faith is nearly always presented in the media as being unclear, weak and contradictory. This leaves our man in the pub with the impression that there is nothing certain about Christianity and so he is better off believing the facts – science! This is a sad distortion of the truth. But one which is made worse by the attitude our society has towards scientists.

Society in previous centuries has been accused of believing everything the church said without stopping to ask questions. In the twentieth century this role has been taken over by the high priests of science! I have been amazed at the way seemingly intelligent people accept without question anything done in the name of science, or said by a scientist. This often means that the general public give great weight to what a scientist says even when he is speaking about things outside his field – just because he wears the label 'scientist'. One of the worst examples of this came during a TV documentary about the beginnings of life on our planet. The presenter explained that in the past people had seen the need for a Great Designer of the universe, but as science probed further and further back in time this was becoming unnecessary. Now this is simply nonsense. Absolute unscientific nonsense! Science is incapable of doing anything more than describing processes – it can never say why these processes occur. Science cannot comment on whether or not God created the world. The presenter was, of course, entitled to his *opinion*. But not his opinion masquerading under the guise of science. The way it came over was to give it all the backing of careful scientific investigation. This is misleading at best, manipulative propaganda at worst. All this means that there is a major difference in the way the general public sees science and the way it is seen by a scientist. Popular opinion may see all kinds of conflict between science and Christianity. Informed scientific opinion is likely to see much less. In general terms, whenever science speaks about areas which are scientific, conflict between it and Christianity is minimal.

What about evolution?

Of all the issues which have caused concern about the relationship between science and faith, evolution has been the most explosive. 'If we evolved from the primeval slime then God didn't make us and the book of Genesis is a fairy tale.' Well, is that true? What is the truth about evolution?

Not all scientists believe it!

This sounds unlikely because the impression we are given is that the entire scientific world believes it and only a few eccentrics or religious cranks would deny it. The fact is that dozens of reputable scientists simply do not believe that the commonly stated evolutionary theory is the best explanation of the facts we have. I would like to quote two of them: Professor H J Lipson (Physicist):

'I think, however, that we must go further than this and admit that the only acceptable explanation is creation. I know that this is anathema to physicists, as indeed it is to me, but we must not reject a theory that we do not like if the experimental evidence supports it.' (H J Lipson, *A Physicist looks at Evolution, Physics Bulletin* No 31, 1980.)

Professor Chandra Wickramasinghe (astronomer):

'The idea that life was put together by random shuffling of constituent molecules can be shown (in the words of Sir Fred Hoyle) to be as ridiculous and improbable as the proposition that a tornado blowing through a junk yard may assemble a Boeing 747. The aircraft had a creator and so might life.'
(*The Lion Handbook of Christian Belief*, Lion.)

Neither of these two men, to my knowledge, are Christians. They are just unconvinced by the scientific evidence for evolution. And there are plenty of other scientists, Christian and non-Christian, who feel the same way. There is no need to feel embarrassed or intellectually inferior if you find creation a more viable option than evolution. It is a perfectly reasonable alternative.

Evolution is not a fact!

It is a scientific theory with, it must be said, some good evidence to support it. Nevertheless it cannot be taught as the truth. Sir Hermann Bondi, internationally acclaimed cosmologist, explains it like this:

> Evolution ' . . . is scientific precisely because it is continually subject to modification and disproof in the light of fresh insights and data accruing in numerous fields of research.
> To teach it dogmatically as fact presents as erroneous a view of science as does the dogmatic teaching of physics or astronomy. If only more teaching of science stressed its human and provisional nature which is its glory!'
> (*The Lion Handbook of Christian Belief*, Lion.)

Science is constantly on the move; refining, correcting and reviewing its theories. Sometimes it has held positions totally contrary to the present ones and may do so again. A new discovery may open the way for a completely different idea from evolution to describe our origins.

Evolution is a description!

This is a vital fact to grasp so that we can understand the limited scope of evolution. Many people, including a large number of Christians, have found it difficult to reconcile their belief in God with the theory of evolution. Some Christians have simply buried their heads in the sand and hoped the issue would go away. Others have come up with ludicrous statements – 'God put fossils in the ground to confuse wicked scientists!' – which are sad reflections of how far frightened people will go. Both these escapist solutions miss the point of evolution being only a description. It cannot *cause* anything. Let me explain.

If we ask the question, 'why did the man fall from the roof?', science can draw on its resources to tell us about the mechanisms involved – the mass of the man, the velocity of the fall, gravitational pull, etc. But this is only a description of what happened. Gravity did not *make* the man fall! To find out the cause we have to ask other questions. Did he slip? Was he pushed? Did he jump? Similarly, evolution is a description of the way life may have started but it cannot explain what made it start and why. Only non-scientific questions can do that. Was it chance? God? Evolution simply cannot say. This means that even if every single piece of current evolutionary theory proved accurate it would not rule God out of the picture.

Of course, some evolutionists do want to rule God out of the picture completely. They want to say that we are evolving morally as a race, moving on from our savage past to a civilized future with no need for a supreme being. Some evolutionists want to use their theory for political ends. (It is fascinating, for example, to discover that the Nazis used it to justify the mass murder of millions of Jews in World War Two!) Whenever people talk like this they are speaking as philosophers or politicians, but not as scientists. No scientific weight can be given to their views. Christians are absolutely opposed to this misuse of science and the views (sometimes called evolutionism) which spring from it. There is, however, no inherent conflict between *scientific* statements about evolution, and Christianity.

True science can have no fundamental conflict with the Christian faith. To try to avoid the claims of Christianity by saying that science has made it redundant or proved it false, is to retreat into illogicality. No, science continues to explore the music of the universe by discovering more and more about the workings of melody, harmony, chord progressions and even the notes themselves. The composer is discovered in a completely different way!

7
What about all the hypocrites?

At a recent Wednesday night meeting at our church I asked people to list the reasons why they felt Christianity was unpopular with the people they worked with. There were over one hundred people at the meeting from a wide variety of backgrounds and occupations. Lots of reasons were given but the most frequently mentioned was the behaviour of Christians. The thrust of the attack was – 'Christianity is great, it's Christians who are a pain in the neck'.

Let's be honest and say that Christianity has its fair share of hypocrites. Every time we see headlines in the Sunday papers like 'Vice vicar in love nest scandal', or read of priests stealing from church funds, or learn that a supposedly born-again Christian celebrity has divorced his wife or cheated the Inland Revenue, we begin to wonder if the whole thing isn't just a farce. Worse still, we may actually know someone in our street who claims to be a Christian but is a bad neighbour and known in the district for his unfriendly manner. Perhaps you work with a Christian who arrives late and leaves early, does a poor job of work and takes things home with him which don't belong to him. All this evidence is beginning to make Christianity seem a bit of a sham! No wonder people say, 'If this is Christianity, I don't want anything to do with it!'

If it is, I don't either! But is it? Are Christians just a bunch of people who talk big but live bad? Before we look at some of the facts behind all this supposed hypocrisy in Christianity let's destroy a couple of myths.

1. Sometimes people accuse the church or individual Christians of hypocrisy, while the accusers assume their own innocence.
This is simply not the case. If a definition of hypocrisy is 'to say one thing and do another', every human being is a hypocrite. Which of us can honestly claim to have never said something we didn't really mean? Or never done something we said we wouldn't? To a greater or lesser extent we are all hypocrites. Unless we are honest enough to admit that, the whole discussion that follows is pointless. When we diagnose hypocrisy as the disease of Christianity it must be with the understanding that we are fellow sufferers!

After all, it's only fair to give some weight to the hypocrisy which Christians see in the non-Christian world. Some people live all their lives with no time for God or his church and then want a priest or minister to give them a Christian funeral – hedging their bets in case there was something in Christianity after all. And what about parents who want their child christened but have no real intention of fulfilling the promises they would make or of attending a church themselves? Or young couples who want to get married in church because it will look nice on the photos but who will make promises to a God they don't really believe in, in a building they don't intend to visit again. Sheer hypocrisy!

All this illustrates how hard it is for any of us to be truly consistent. Yes, some Christians are hypocrites; but the church has not cornered the market in hypocrisy; we are all guilty.

2. Hypocrisy is often confused with deliberate manipulation.
I suppose that the arena in which hypocrisy is most common
is politics. The average person takes with a pinch of salt
what politicans say in the run-up to an election – we assume
that they will promise almost anything to get elected, and
once they are, will conveniently forget any policy which is
awkward to put into practice. Now, whether this is true of
every politician or not, as a society we have tended to equate
this deliberate distortion of what someone *really* thinks (in
order to achieve the goal of election) with hypocrisy. 'He
never really meant any of that stuff he said; he'd say
anything to become an MP.' And there are other examples
of this kind of hypocrisy. The man at your door offers to
concrete your drive. You never see him or your deposit
again. People who sell phoney investment deals to
pensioners. 'This car has only had one careful old lady
owner' type of car salesman. There are always going to be
people willing to lie deliberately to achieve their own ends.

But this kind of hypocrisy (cynical manipulation) is very rare indeed among Christians. Their hypocrisy is usually to be equated with failure. The vicar who interferes with little boys, the cantankerous Christian boss, the priest who ends up in bed with the choir mistress – none of these people planned this from the beginning as their goal in life. They have not wilfully deceived, rather they have tragically failed. They cannot be condemned with the same venom as the con-men described above.

None of this excuses their behaviour, of course. They claimed to live by a set of standards (the Christian faith) and did not do it. They are hypocrites. But not hypocrites of the manipulating kind, rather the failure kind. Any reasonable person would want to condemn both kinds of hypocrisy; however, the first deserves our anger and the second our pity.

Now let's tackle head-on this 'Christians are hypocrites' business. I am going to make what I believe are five factual statements to help us decide whether to accept or reject Christianity on the basis of the way some Christians behave.

Christians are not always Christians!

The word 'Christian' is used in so many ways these days it is hard to know what it means. There are political parties called 'Christian Democratic', a fighting unit in the Middle East called the 'Christian Militia' and a church known to me where they have a Christian cabaret!

People who call themselves Christians may not actually be Christians; and if they are not it would hardly be fair to judge real Christians by what these pretend Christians say or do. For example, over the last few years one man has stood for more elections than anyone else. He is a member of the 'Monster Raving Loony' party and calls himself Lord David Sutch. His behaviour and speeches are colourful, to say the least! But if people started to draw the conclusion that all members of the aristocracy acted like this, a real Lord would be quick to point out that Lord Sutch was no such thing! So it is only fair to make a judgment on Christianity on the basis of how real Christians behave.

Someone may go to church, be friendly and honest and believe in God, but still not be a Christian. The Bible is quite clear about this. A Christian is someone who has a personal relationship with God; an experience so profound that it is sometimes described as being born all over again. Many accusations of hypocrisy are levelled at people who are Christians in name only, not at those in whom the revolution of meeting Jesus has taken place.

Imagine how peeved you would be if you had worked for five years to gain a doctorate degree and someone else had written to Micky Mouse University in America and got a doctorate in the same subject for ten dollars and the tops from three packets of cornflakes. Imagine how angry you would feel if it was assumed you both had the same level of learning. Christians sometimes feel very much like this; frustrated at being judged on the basis of those who share our name, but not the reality of our experience.

This information (that all those who call themselves Christians are not necessarily real Christians) can come as quite a shock if we have glibly assumed what people claimed about themselves to be true. But should we be so surprised? Our society is becoming expert at substituting plastic for the genuine article: soya products for meat, dream topping for cream, and—more seriously—lust for love, charity for compassion. Only the discerning can tell they are being deceived. We must not reject a substitute Christianity imagining we have rejected the real thing. We must ask ourselves if the behaviour we are condeming as hypocrisy has been committed by real Christians or by an extremely plausible imitation of the real thing. The point at stake here is this: can we dismiss Christians as hypocrites because some people who call themselves Christians behave badly? I think not.

Over the last few years, violence at football matches has resulted in English clubs being banned from European competition. What was once a family afternoon out has become a venue for the brave or reckless. Manager after manager and chairman after chairman, has spoken out against the hooligan element masquerading as supporters. The fact is that the trouble-makers look like real supporters, sing the same songs and go to the same venue – yet are condemned by everyone for not being real supporters. It would take a strange logic to come up with the conclusion that football was a bad game or that there were no genuine fans just because some people went to the ground for fighting, not football!

It would be equally illogical to judge Christianity as a whole because so-called Christians acted wrongly, or to condemn genuine fans of Christianity because of what others who appear like us, do. They may look like us, sing the same songs, even attend the same church. Only if they have had an encounter with Jesus are they really Christians. Of course, we must be honest enough to admit that even real Christians can be hypocrites. When they are it is perfectly reasonable to question their sincerity and the validity of the Christian faith as a whole. However, when we do that we come up against some other facts which we have to wrestle with.

Some non-Christians behave better than Christians

True! If by this we mean that we know some non-Christians who are nicer, kinder and more helpful than some Christians. We may even feel that we are better people than some Christians we know – we could well be! Sometimes those arguing against the Christian faith take the next steps in the argument like this . . .

'I'm not a hypocrite like Joe Christian. He takes things from work (or beats his wife, etc.) and I am far too honest to do that. My behaviour is better than his, so it's likely his Christianity isn't any good; it certainly doesn't help him much, so I don't see why I should need it either.'

On the face of it this sounds extremely reasonable. The criticism of Joe involves two basic ideas: his hypocrisy discredits his Christianity (see next section) and the *difference* in our behaviour discredits his Christianity. But wait a minute, is it fair for us to compare ourselves with Joe in such a simple way? What if Joe is under massive pressure we know nothing about? Close to the poverty line? Near to a nervous breakdown? Living with a terminally ill child to look after? Now none of this would excuse Joe's behaviour or make it right, but it might help explain it. What these questions do highlight is the great difficulty in making judgments on other people's lives without knowing all the facts. The only safe question is whether or not Joe is a better person now *than he would have been if he had not become a Christian*. For example, if Joe had been a psychopathic killer and now only takes paper clips from work, I'd say a good case could be made for the effectiveness of his Christianity!

This leads us to clarify what Joe is claiming as a Christian. He is *not* claiming to be perfect but just forgiven and improving! He is going to make mistakes and fall flat on his face. But because of God's power inside him he is slowly becoming more like the Jesus he follows and less like the hypocritical Joe he was, and sometimes still is. Knowing what someone has come from does make a tremendous difference to the way we relate to them. At first sight, you would treat a twenty-stone man recommending his diet to you as a bit of a joke. If you found out he used to be thirty stone you might think again, even if you only weigh twelve stone. Some Christians are like this. They have got a long way to go but they are moving in the right direction.

This is, in fact, exactly what Christians say. Let's put the words in Joe's mouth:

'I know I sometimes take things from work. I'm sorry, and know I shouldn't do it. I am better than I was though. I'm not trying to make excuses, but I've taken a step in the right direction. I feel Jesus has forgiven me, but I'm not perfect – just forgiven and improving!

So, just because my behaviour is better than Joe's doesn't discredit his Christianity. But that leads us to another question, and the third statement.

Hypocrisy doesn't discredit Christianity

It is perfectly reasonable to be annoyed by hypocrisy. But is it reasonable to go beyond anger to a rejection of the faith which the hypocritical person holds?

Last winter, during a particularly cold spell I came downstairs to discover our pipes had frozen. After an initial dribble there was not a drop of water in the entire house. Eventually, after a day without water, the offending pipe was discovered and warmed up. I didn't realize how much water we used until the day we couldn't get any! All this was very frustrating, but can you imagine me saying, 'That's it, I'm disgusted! I don't want anything to do with water ever again. I'll wash with milk . . . I'll . . . I'll . . . I'll never trust water again!' Anyone who reasons like this could expect a visit from a couple of men in white coats! We all know that there is absolutely nothing wrong with the water, just a defect in the means of getting it to us.

In the same way, God has given his message to people (Christians) and has told them to pass it on to others. They often fail to pass it on; their lives get clogged up with all sorts of rubbish, and God's love has a hard time getting through to anyone else. However, to blame God for this or to imagine that *he* has somehow been discredited is as illogical as refusing to use the water. We cannot, reasonably, dismiss Christianity because some of the people through whom it passes are 'defective pipes'. Power failures don't discredit electricity; car breakdowns don't mean we never drive again. In all these cases, the principle remains valid even when an expression of the principle fails. If anyone doubted the existence or usefulness of electricity just because they have an old radio that doesn't work, we would doubt their sanity; yet people come to precisely this conclusion about Christianity on the basis of power failure among some

Christians. There is absolutely nothing wrong with their power *supply*, they just seem to have faulty connections.

We ought not to leave this section without saying that although hypocrisy gives us no logical reason for rejecting Christianity, it does make us sceptical on emotional grounds. This is what makes it so dangerous; we see hypocrisy and instinctively feel something is wrong. It's a little like watching a bald man selling hair restorer: something is not quite right; we sense an inconsistency. Emotionally we reject the whole thing as fake. But what if the plain fact was that he enjoyed being bald, or had not got round to using the restorer yet? The truth is his baldness tells us absolutely nothing about whether the hair restorer works or not, but it makes us feel uneasy with his claim. The only way to know for sure is to try it for ourselves and see. Inconsistent and hypocritical Christians do make it harder for us to believe that their message works; but the only real test of its validity is for us to explore its claims for ourselves.

So far in this chapter we have tried to explain some of the things it is reasonable to say about Christians who are hypocrites. (And some of the things which it is not!) The next two sections look at some of the positive statements Christians can make about hypocrisy.

There are only fakes of valuable things

A hypocrite is a fake, someone who claims to be something different from what he is. But have you noticed that there are only fakes of things of value? Rembrandts are copied because the originals are so highly valued. No forger on earth would waste time trying to produce an exact copy of the doodles I'm doing while writing this book! The originals just aren't worth anything! Yet any art gallery would confirm that the more famous the painter the more alert they have to be for forgeries. And so with Christianity. Anything that claims to be this wonderful is bound to suffer from imitations.

In both cases the issue is cost. If you really want a Picasso in your living room you may settle for a reproduction because it's cheaper. Many people settle for something that looks like Christianity because they're not prepared to pay the cost involved in the real thing. The presence of hypocrisy does seem to imply a genuinely valuable faith behind it. After all, you can't have a fake without an original. Ever seen a fake £11 note? Of course not! Because the real thing doesn't exist. If there are fake Rembrandts there must be real ones. If there are fake fivers there must be real ones and, if there are fake Christians . . . !! Hypocrisy certainly discredits individual Christians but it does seem to point beyond the individual to a valuable and genuine faith.

Jesus hates hypocrisy

It is important to finish the chapter by making clear that none of the arguments we have used in any way excuses the hypocrisy itself. All true Christians hate hypocrisy because Jesus hated it. Let's not be in any doubt just how vigorously the founder of Christianity opposed hypocrisy of every kind. Listen to these words from 'Gentle Jesus meek and mild'. They are addressed to a group of religious leaders.

> 'You religious leaders are hypocrites! You pretend to be holy and you say long prayers in public; but behind the scenes you throw innocent widows out of their homes. You are sons of hell and anyone you convert becomes twice as bad as you under your influence. You are blind guides and fools; clean on the outside, dirty where it counts on the inside, hypocrites! You are greedy, extortionate, legalistic, deceitful . . . more like snakes than the shepherds you are supposed to be!'[7]

Talk about angry – we are talking volcanic! Anything that smacks of double standards is exposed for what it is by Jesus. He hated hypocrisy then and he hates it now. Anyone who is against hypocrisy has an ally in Jesus of Nazareth. The good news for all of us is that he hates hypocrisy . . . but can find it in his heart to love hypocrites.

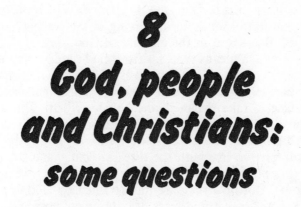

8
God, people and Christians:
some questions

How can a God of love send people to hell?

Hell means total separation from everything good. The flames described in the Bible may be picture language, but the reality they represent is no figment of the imagination. One of the reasons it exists is because of the seriousness with which God takes the decisions of men and women. If we choose to reject him and his offer of life, with his way of escape from all the dirtiness in the world, he refuses to overrule our decision. He won't force us to accept his love, because that would rob us of the privilege of choice and make us mere robots. So we do have to take the consequences of our decisions. Which means by choosing to live without God we have indeed *chosen to live without God* — now and for ever.

And it is no use asking why we can't choose to live without God in this life, but choose to live with him in the next. The question completely misses the point about the radical nature of the choice. It's as if we wanted to choose not to have any children of our own and then at the age of eighty to change our mind and want to have grown-up children around to look after us. It's too late; our earlier decision has had inevitable consequences. So it is with our decision about God. There comes a point (death) when our earlier decision is too far gone to change. Which means we have chosen to spend eternity living in the presence of our own sinfulness and in the absence of God.

All of which means that, far from God sending us to hell, we seem to be sending ourselves. After all, it would be most unreasonable to blame the doctor for our ill health if we refuse to take the medicine he prescribed! The divine doctor has diagnosed the sin-sickness of mankind and offered a forgiveness-cure. If we refuse or ignore the offer we will have to live with the disease. And that's what hell is: living after death with all our worst traits still raging inside us. But now they are unrestrained by God or social convention – a seething mass of unforgiven vices and unresolved conflicts. God does not want anyone to go to hell and so he has prepared a way for mankind to escape its horrors. He is in the business of getting people into heaven not sending them to hell!

Isn't Christianity just a psychological crutch?

No!
Not if you mean that the faith a Christian has is just wishful thinking, all in the mind. As if we can dismiss his faith by implying that in some way he *needs* to believe it, and therefore does. This is a very dangerous argument indeed – for the one who uses it! Take a double-edged knife, place your thumb over one of the sharp edges and put the other on a

piece of wood. As you push hard the wood is cut. So is your thumb! The knife, like the argument above, cuts both ways. After all, the Christian could argue that an atheist does not believe in God in the same way – he believes there is no God so that he doesn't have to bother about his commands. Hey presto, there is no God! But this belief is equally 'all in the mind'.

No!
Not if you mean Christian experience is *just* psychological. It does of course involve psychological aspects of our lives. It involves our mind, emotions and will. But that is not the whole story. For example, a scientist could describe cricket in terms of velocity, mass, density and distance. He could

be exhaustive in defining every principle involved. Still he could not say that cricket is just a series of principles in physics! There are other dimensions – the rules of the game, winning and competing, and so on. Christian conversion is like this. It *is* psychological. But when you have said this you have only said one small part of what needs to be said.

No!
Not if you mean Christianity is a crutch like alcohol or drugs. Something to help the weak through tough situations, as if Christians are basically failures as people and need something to help them get by. 'Is Christianity *true?*' is the vital question. (As a quadriplegic girl named Joni said, 'I believe in Jesus not because it is easy but because it is true.') If it isn't it will be useless as a crutch. At least alcohol works even if only for a short time. If Christianity was false it would be a useless crutch. If it's true, it's a cure not a crutch.

Yes!
If you mean Christianity does help people through tough times and over difficulties. Yes, if you mean it's a source of strength and comfort to thousands.

Yes
If you mean it provides a rock of unchanging certainty in an ever-changing world!

Aren't Christians narrow minded?
Yes, it has to be admitted that some Christians are locked into a series of petty rules and regulations that have more to do with tradition than the teaching of Jesus. But if you mean that some of the teaching of Christianity seems narrow and restrictive (eg 'sex outside marriage is wrong') then a couple of things need to be said.

Firstly, these seeming restrictions aren't half as narrow from the inside as they appear from the outside. When I first went to the House of Commons, I was shown round to what appeared to be a side entrance. This door was so narrow that you had to enter in single file. It was so unimposing! Do our MP's really meet in a poky old house? Once you get in, the change is remarkable. Majestic archways, huge halls and miles of corridors. From the outside – small and unimpressive, from the inside – huge and spacious. Similarly, when we become Christians the teaching which looked so restrictive is in fact quite different. Christians don't feel restricted by the Bible's teaching about sex – its very narrowness gives real security to marriage and the freedom to develop a meaningful sex life with a permanent partner you can trust.

When you contrast this with the broad teaching of our permissive society, we are beginning to discover that this 'freedom' means a freedom to break up someone else's marriage, cheapen relationships, hurt members of our own family, bring up a child alone . . . the list of hurts this freedom has caused could go on and on. Not to mention the freedom to get VD, herpes or AIDS! Compared with all this the Christian's narrowness seems a pretty good deal!

Secondly, sometimes narrow-mindedness is just wisdom with a different hat on. Why don't we stop being so narrow-minded about our driving habits? 'How dare they restrict our freedom like this! Drive on any side of the road you want to, stop on green, go on red; when you next go south on the motorway, use the north-bound carriageway. This is your right!' Of course, if you choose to exercise your right you will soon be dead right!

We all know that these rules, although we may resent them at times, are for our own safety and the safety of fellow travellers. Christians see God's rules in the same way – for our protection and best interest, not to cramp our style.

What about those who haven't heard?

It really doesn't seem fair that God should judge people when they have not had the chance to hear about Jesus. Well, let's get one thing clear from the start, God *is* going to act fairly. That's his nature – just, fair and compassionate. This much is guaranteed: when every human being comes face to face with their creator, no one will be able to complain that they got a raw deal.

God has given two clues about himself to every person on earth. The first is the world about us – its beauty, order and design. Live in my house while I am away and my books, tapes and the state of my garden will tell you a great deal about me, even though we may never have met. Live in God's world and the discerning person will notice the marks of his ownership everywhere. The second is the conscience in all of us: that inner voice that keeps us uncomfortable when we do what we know to be wrong. It points out that we can't even live up to our own standards. It is a constant reminder, put there by God, that we need help to become the people we would like to be.

Unfortunately, nobody has ever lived up to their own standards, let alone God's. And so Jesus had to come to give us a new power to do the right thing. There is no way to get this power except through the death and resurrection of Jesus. However, this does not necessarily mean that an individual needs to be aware of this action on his behalf, to receive its benefit. For example, when slavery was abolished in the British empire in 1833, thousands of men and women in Africa were made safe from the threat of abduction and captivity. Many of them knew nothing about the British Government and even less about the act of Parliament which guaranteed their freedom! Despite this ignorance, they enjoyed the freedom the act obtained for them. Any person anywhere who is really sorry for the wrong in their lives and throws themselves completely on God's mercy for their salvation can enjoy the benefits of the Christian message, even without knowing the facts about the death and resurrection of Jesus.

What about those who can't hear?

This question is similar to the last. Usually people want to include in this question two different groups – those who were born before Jesus came and those who do not have the capacity to understand the Christian message. (Such as children who die in infancy, the severely mentally retarded.)

1. Throughout the Bible the way to God is the same – by faith in God's mercy; not, even in the Old Testament, by keeping the commandments. All the ancient heroes of the Bible who are said to have pleased God, did so by faith. He accepted their faith on the basis of what Jesus was going to do. They enjoyed the benefits of Jesus' death and resurrection, even though it had not yet happened. I may, for example, get my wife a gift on the strength of a pay rise I have been promised. She experiences the benefit of the increase before I get the money, because I know it's coming! Similarly, God chose to accept people in Old Testament times on the strength of what he knew was coming, in response to their faith.

2. People who don't have the ability to understand the Christian message will not be judged as if they did! God is perfectly fair and understands their limitations better than we do. They will not be automatically damned because of their inability to grasp the message. The Bible does, however, indicate clearly the people who *are* going to be judged – those who reject the message, and those who hear it and never get round to making a decision about it! If you are reading this book, you have the capacity to understand the facts about Jesus Christ. Very young babies and people with terribly damaged minds would seem incapable of either the rejection or the delaying tactics the Bible so strongly condemns.

God does not want *anyone* to be lost and that he is deeply concerned about every human being. When he expresses special concern for the weak and defenceless in society we can be certain that he has tragic circumstances, like the death of a baby, near to his heart. We know he will do the just and fair thing.

What about all the denominations?

The implication behind this question is usually that there are so many different ones to choose from, how can we possibly know which is right? Why don't all Christians believe the same things?

We ought to start by saying that the differences between denominations are not as fundamental as some people think. The difference between Buddhism and Christianity is like the difference between chalk and cheese. In comparison, the difference between Baptist and Methodist is like Cheddar and Edam. Whatever the denomination, all true believers have a fundamental unity with all other true believers. This means that they are Christians first and Anglicans (for example) second. The absolutely crucial questions have nothing to do with which denomination you belong to.

The most obvious differences are to do with the form the Sunday service takes. Some are very quiet, some follow a set pattern, others never do the same thing two weeks running. Some ministers wear robes, some a suit, others jeans! But behind all these differences lie other, more complex areas of disagreement. Sometimes it's a matter of giving one of the truths in the Bible a special emphasis; sometimes a sincere disagreement about what the Bible actually means. Occasionally, it's an accident of history where a personal squabble between two leaders has hardened over the years into rival groupings. Whatever the reasons, we can't escape the fact that there are more denominations around than ever before.

But we must not make the mistake of rejecting Christianity because there are so many churches to choose from. That would be as absurd as giving up food because we were bewildered by the variety of supermarkets. Let's make two observations for the discerning church 'shopper':

1. All true Christians are agreed on the fundamentals of the faith. So much so that they could happily meet in one another's homes and talk about Jesus without the denomination question ever arising. Even if there were a million denominations nothing could alter the basis of their faith – Jesus Christ.

2. There are really dead churches in every denomination. So don't choose a local church just because it is linked with a denomination you like. Check a few out and go to one where they talk about Jesus, believe in the Bible and you sense something special during the service. And by the way, there won't be any denominations in heaven. So don't worry about them too much down here!

Can you prove that Christianity is true?

That depends on the kind of proof you are looking for. The Christian faith can't be examined in a laboratory. But then the really important things are all like this – love, peace, friendship, fun; none of these can be placed under a microscope. In fact we accept the vast majority of things in our lives without any strictly scientific proof.

But there is another kind of proof which we use all the time, almost without thinking about it. We sometimes call this 'legal' proof and it rests on two levels of enquiry: eyewitness accounts, and supporting evidence. If I wanted to prove where I went on holiday I would produce supporting evidence like my passport with a country's stamp in it, my photos and the bill for the hotel room. In addition, I would talk about an overgrown cliff walk, an unbelievably grubby corner café and a newly painted pier; all this indicating that I had actually seen the place with my own eyes. Now Christianity is open to this kind of proof. I will have to conduct my own defence and it goes something like this:

'I have examined as much of the supporting evidence that I could lay my hands on, the main document being the Bible. I have found it to be thoroughly reliable. I have had the experience which the book offers and can now talk about things in a way which would simply be impossible if I had not seen this truth for myself. On the basis of the supporting evidence (the Bible and the experience of others) and what I have experienced personally, I have come to the conclusion that Christianity is true.'

And we can all prove Christianity for ourselves by the same method. Examine the supporting evidence as honestly as possible. Then be prepared to accept God's offer. When you do, something happens that opens your eyes to a whole new world. A marvellous, exciting (and demanding!) world filled with new things from horizon to horizon. Enjoy the view.

Note: Collecting 'legal' proof takes time. You are not going to prove or disprove Christianity in ten minutes. Such a crucial issue deserves careful and thoughtful enquiry.

Isn't the church out of date and out of touch?

Sometimes! A trip to church can be like experiencing a time warp, finding yourself back in the last century. To boldly go where no man would want to bother going! Some churches do give every appearance of belonging to our history books rather than having any relevance today. When you get inside you could be forgiven for thinking that you had wandered into a museum by mistake. Once the service begins you may be attacked by 'Thees' and 'Thous', confused by instructions to 'approach the throne of grace' (whoever she is!) and asked to sing about the 'waste places of Jerusalem breaking forth with joy.' No wonder it all seems out of date and irrelevant.

Wait a minute though, lots of churches are not like this any more; some big changes have happened in the last few years. Some of the churches in your area will be a hundred times more up-to-date than you remember, if you last went as a child. You may well understand, and relate to, more than you think.

Talking of understanding, Christians do have their own

special vocabulary. I used to think that chips had something to do with fish, a byte was what you got from a mosquito and software was an old woolly jumper! But now I know it's computer talk, a specialized language to explain a specific activity. In Christianity we have words like 'faith' and 'salvation' which we cannot do without. These words are not old-fashioned, just part of the technical language of the Christian faith. Once you get the hang of the terms, things become much clearer.

The other thing to remember is this. Just because something is old doesn't necessarily mean it is old-fashioned. Breathing and eating have been around since the creation of man and not many of us are going to stop doing either merely because they have been happening a long time. In fact, in some ways, the reverse is true. Haven't all things of real value been around for aeons – love, peace, friendship? Christianity is old in the sense that its values are permanent. Most of us would rather base our lives on this than on some trendy new idea which will be out of date itself within months.

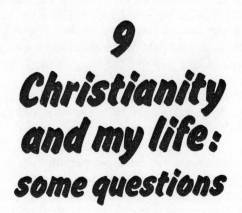

9
Christianity and my life: some questions

Can't I live a good life without being a Christian?

Yes!
If you mean 'Can non-Christians do kind and helpful things for others?' Many people with no Christian faith at all work for charities, give time and money to needy causes and are good neighbours. You don't need to be a Christian to help an old lady across the road.

No!
Not if you mean 'Can I be as good as it is possible for me to be, without being a Christian?' However good any of us are, none of us would claim to be perfect. So there is always room for improvement. Jesus Christ offers an inner strength to make us better people. If we want to be good people, why on earth would we turn down his offer of help? Even if you are very good indeed, there is no area which would not be improved by knowing Jesus.

No!

Not if you mean 'good enough for God'. However good we may be we cannot meet God's 'goodness standard'. Let's imagine a competition to jump across the English Channel. The first competitor, a seventy-year-old alcoholic, manages three feet. His rival, a twenty-year-old decathlon champion, manages twenty-five feet. He is vastly superior to his fellow competitor, but this difference pales into insignificance compared with the twenty-two miles they would need to jump to get all the way across! God's 'goodness standard' is Jesus Christ. Compared with him the very best of us fails abysmally. And of course the very worst fail too.

This means that good and bad people need Jesus. Good people may feel they need him a little less, but they *need* him just the same. The difference between good and bad people is measured in 'feet'; between good people and Jesus it is measured in 'miles'! So it's no good claiming to be 'as good as the next man' or 'better than those people from the church', or to say you 'wouldn't harm a soul', even if every word of it is true. The rich young ruler in the Bible could say all those things and he still went away from Jesus a sad and unfulfilled man (Luke 18:18–24).

It is right to do good deeds. Our world needs more people who give selflessly of their time and money to help others. But if we are counting on our goodness to earn God's approval we are in for a nasty shock. No one is good enough.

Can't I be a Christian without going to church?

Well, yes, it is possible, but you could also survive on chocolate cake and Pepsi, make love in a bed of nettles or sun-bathe in the Antarctic! These activities are all possible but highly undesirable. No one would view them as being the best options available. Similarly, we have to say that the best option for a Christian is to be part of a local church. Why?

Because real Christians need to.
Before you become a Christian, going to church regularly seems like a pretty stiff requirement. When you are one, you soon see the immense value of being with other Christians – to learn together and to encourage one another. Without this kind of support our faith would struggle to survive. Indeed it would be questionable whether we were real Christians at all. Footballers need a team. However much they practice on their own, even if they can balance the ball on their nose or kick it into a net half a mile away, they still need a team to be real footballers. Football is a team game. So is Christianity.

Because real Christians want to.
It's very hard to describe, but nothing on earth can replace the sense of God's presence when Christians get together for worship. Of course, some times in church are better than others – but there is always the potential for another encounter with our God. Something inside us urges us to be with God's people.

Because real Christians want the best.
The original question seems to imply, 'Can I get away with not going to church?' Yes, is the answer, but is it the best thing for a Christian? How much can you take out of a car before it stops being a car? Radio, seat covers, and ashtray – no problem. Horn, indicators and headlights – possibly. Brakes, tyres and engine? At some point it ceases to be a car, but long before then it ceases to be a very good car.

There are lots of things you can get away with doing as a Christian – sooner or later you reach the point where you can't be one at all. However, long before then you have reached the point of not being a very good Christian. Why settle for mediocrity? Why not go for the best? As a Christian that will mean regular church attendance.

Won't becoming a Christian make me boring?

I have heard people talk about their decision to become Christians as if this involved a change from an exciting life to one which has all the thrills of watching paint dry! 'I used to go to parties every night, had loads of girls, life was a blast. Then . . . (adopting serious tone and expression) I became a Christian. Now I don't do any of the stuff I used to do. I go to prayer meetings, read my Bible and pick up old ladies for church!' Certainly sounds dull! But wait a minute . . .

Being a Christian is about following Jesus and becoming like him. There is no way Jesus could be described as boring. He gave up the security of a nine-to-five job as a carpenter at the age of thirty, gathered a bunch of half-educated oddballs around him, and set off on a three year walk round Palestine. He was regularly misunderstood, often without a bed for the night and eventually betrayed by a close associate. This led to a bloody and cruel death. During his life he became known for practising medicine without a licence, drawing large crowds, doing amazing things with fish and bread and making outrageous statements about following him and living for ever! This character is anything *but* boring and his followers are offered the same new dimension of living. Some Christians lock this new life up tight within them and miss some of its exciting dimensions, but if we let this Jesus-life have full control, our lives need never be dull.

The other important thing to remember when you see Christians doing things which seem dull and uninteresting, compared with your current lifestyle, is this. When you become a Christian the kind of thing you enjoy changes.

When I was a child my dad would cross his legs, sit me on his foot and bounce me up and down. I wanted to do this again and again. It was great! It will come as no surprise to you that I haven't wanted to do this for years – nor for that matter has my father! I now enjoy other things. When you become a Christian some of the things you used to do seem unattractive, even boring, in comparison with what you have available to you now.

I'm happy as I am; I don't need to change.

'Things are going well for me, thank you. I have my little ups and downs but basically life is fine just the way it is. Why should I change what I believe?' Sometimes we do arrive at a settled lifestyle: no money worries, a comfortable home and a secure job. In situations like this, Christianity seems irrelevant at best and interfering at worst.

Of course, while *you* may be happy as you are, others may not be so sure. Your wife may want to see change in you and so may your boss. Ask your children (or parents) if they are happy with the way you are. This statement could just be the selfish assertion 'Blow you Jack, I'm all right!' In which case you most certainly do need to change!

But let's, for argument's sake, say that you are happy as you are and that those around you seem to agree. Could it be that your satisfaction with yourself is based on an inadequate view of happiness? I mean, if you had only ever had dry toast you would not be able to imagine the delights of Black Forest gateau or strawberries and cream! Christians maintain that once you have discovered Christianity, everything else is dry toast! And so to say that you are happy as you are is to rob yourself of whole new vistas of fulfilment. Jesus said that he had come to bring a new, richer quality of life. He keeps his promise.

Could it also be that your happiness is based on ignorance of the real situation? What if you knew that at this moment of happiness the first cancerous cell had appeared in your body? You would change your eating habits, take medication or do anything else the doctor suggested. You would be stupid to say that you were not going to change anything because you felt happy. Sin, the Bible says, is an even more deadly disease which affects all of us. It is silently growing away inside us and, if it continues, will prove eternally fatal. No wonder Christians think that a happiness which has not come to terms with this problem is very superficial. After all, an ostrich with its head in the sand may be happy, but is it safe?

How can one man's death, so long ago, possibly affect me?

Sometimes people are unable to see how a man being killed nearly two thousand years ago can possibly affect them today. The death of a Judean carpenter in some obscure corner of the world hardly seems likely to make the nine o'clock news, never mind be anything to do with me hundreds of years later.

On June 28th, 1914, an Austrian archduke was killed by a schoolboy. His tragic death was reported but its significance completely overlooked. Within six weeks it became clear that it had been the fuse which triggered off World War One! Millions were killed or horribly injured and the map of Europe was decisively altered. The whole history of the world was changed by that assassination in Sarejevo. In a much more profound way the death of Jesus affected all of us. The presence of the church, the Bible, our calendar –

and much more – highlights the impact he made. Billions remember his death every Easter and millions of those claim that his death has changed them personally.

But how? For Christians Jesus is not just a dead hero but a Saviour. Some years ago a plane crashed into an ice-cold river. Television cameras recorded the heroic attempts of one man to help with the rescue by plunging into the river to drag survivors from the wreckage. After one person had been pulled to safety he returned for another. He never came back to the shore. Now for thousands watching on television that man was a hero, but for the person he rescued he was much, much more. He was a saviour. The same is true about every Christian's attitude to Jesus. He gave his life so that we could live. Because of the wrong we do, we deserve to be punished. But, instead, Jesus took that punishment for us so we don't need to be punished after all. No wonder we are grateful to Jesus for dying in our place.

The benefits of this event all those years ago come to us through the terms of a will. Jesus, in his will, left forgiveness and eternal life to everyone who wanted it and who would fulfil certain conditions. We all know that a will does not come into effect until after the person has died. So it is only because Jesus has died that we can claim our legacy. And what a great inheritance it is!

It's all right for you, but not for me

Thousands of Christians have had this said to them. Usually it puts a stop to any discussion about faith in Jesus. But it shouldn't. It's yet another of those statements which sound sensible but actually holds as much water as a sieve. Let's have a look at three of the holes.

It's illogical

If Christianity is wrong then you ought not to be saying that it's all right for me. The Christian faith makes major demands. If it is wrong I am wasting lots of valuable time at church and Christian events, being cheated out of a quite a sizable proportion of my income and generally throwing my life away on a worthless cause. What kind of friend are you, saying it's OK if I believe all this nonsense?!

And if Christianity is true, the statement is equally illogical. People often say it as if they were comparing cars. 'I know you are really keen on your Jaguar but I'm perfectly happy with my Ford.' Behind this attitude lies a complete misunderstanding about the nature of Christianity. Christianity is either true or false. This means it is either true for both of us or neither of us. We can illustrate the logical absurdity of this statement by making the subject 'America'. 'It's all right for you to believe in America, but it's not for me.' America is either a place on planet Earth or it isn't. Whether you believe it or not won't change the facts! One of us is wrong.

It's dangerous

Christianity is basically a rescue operation. It claims to have diagnosed mankind's basic disease (sin) and is offering a course of treatment for its cure. Millions are taking the medicine; it sometimes takes a while to work and the improvement is not always spectacular. But are you really in a position to think of yourself as a special case? 'The cure is OK for you, but I'd rather not bother with it', hardly sounds a safe and sensible response to Christianity.

It's silly!

The Christian faith offers joy and peace. Are you seriously saying it is all right for me to have this but you don't want it? It offers a relationship with God, eternal joy and a unique quality of life here on earth. You don't want a good time when you die? Or even right now?

If you think Christianity is *wrong*, say so! But if you *really* think it's all right for me you are surely being illogical, dangerous and silly to reject it.

But I am already a Christian!

If you really are a Christian, that's great. But how do you know you are a Christian? What is it that makes you think you are? Here are a few of the most common reasons people give to support their claim to be a Christian.

'I go to church.'

Many people go to church to worship God, but many others go out of habit, to be seen by the right people or to please the wife! Lots of young people go because they can't get out of it. But going to a sports centre doesn't make you a sportsman – you have to get changed and do something. Going to church doesn't make you a Christian – you have to be changed and start to behave like one.

'I was born a Christian . . .

. . . in a Christian country', the argument usually continues. Sorry, being born in a garage wouldn't make you a car! No one is born a Christian any more than anyone is born with pierced ears. Both things involve a definite decision on our part.

'I believe in God.'

So does the devil and it would be difficult to describe him as a Christian! So do thousands of Muslims and they would never dream of describing themselves as Christians.

Added to these three could be lots of others: I pray, I give money to charity, I am basically a nice person . . . and so on. At the heart of the problem is confusion about what a Christian really is. Your definition may be just as good as mine. Compared with God's definition, none of our definitions matter too much. If you have a Bible handy you might want to look up these verses. A Christian . . .

- Recognizes they need help – Romans 3:23.
- Is ready to turn their back on everything they know to be wrong – Acts 2:38.
- Trusts in Jesus to put things right – 1 Peter 2:24.
- Invites Jesus to be in charge of their life – John 1:12.

Of course there are lots more things involved in living the Christian life but these steps summarize the way to become one. So, am I really a Christian?

10
Does it make sense?

If we are honest we don't always find it easy to make sense of our lives. What are we here for, and why? What's the point of it all? Why can't we sort out the mess the world is in? We seem to stagger from one crisis to the next and a lasting solution is as elusive as the gold at the end of the rainbow. In theory, we all ought to be able to live together in harmony; but in practice we don't. The confusion on our planet reminds me of Lewis Carol's mock poem, *Jaberwocky:*

> 'Twas brillig, and the slithy toves
> Did gyre and gimble in the wabe;
> All mimsy were the borogoves,
> And the mome raths outgrabe.

That's how the first verse goes. It rhymes, flows well and sounds impressive. But it's nonsense; the words don't mean anything. Many of our individual lives are like this. Superficially everything in the garden is lovely, but a closer examination reveals huge marshes of meaninglessness, clumps of contradiction and wodges of the weed confusion. Very few people are prepared to be as brutally honest as this when looking at their lives. But we need to be if we want to discover the truth about ourselves as individuals and as a world. This really is the crunch for all thinking people – are we prepared to weigh all the evidence honestly and follow the facts wherever they lead?

Let's summarize the situation so far. All the previous chapters have dealt with specific questions often used to attack Christianity. I hope, even if you don't agree with all the answers, that you can see that Christians have logical, reasonable grounds for believing the things they do. It's not just some wild, irrational leap of faith. In fact, the Christian faith cannot only give answers to these questions but it can also provide a sensible, cohesive explanation of why things are as they are in our world.

C S Lewis, a writer and scholar, explained this by saying that he believed in Christianity in the same way that he believed in the sun: not only because he could see it, but also because by its light he could see everything else. He believed in Christianity not just because it seemed true in itself but also because in the light of its teaching all other issues in life made more sense. Generations of Christians have found this to be true. Let's look at three issues which affect us all, and see what a Christian makes of them.

Right and wrong

Inside all of us is a sense that some things are right and some are wrong. But how did we get this sense? Christians say that as God made us in his image it's not surprising that we reflect his values. It's as if there were a small deposit of God in us acting like an inner compass; one direction is right, the opposite is wrong. He put it there to give us an inner guide-line on how to behave. If we don't want to accept this explanation, what are the alternatives?

Some say that right and wrong are decided by the society we live in. They argue, for example, that in Britain it's perfectly all right to kill cows and eat them, but a Hindu society would think that was very wrong. But this argument fails to take into account the *basic* agreement between right and wrong across cultural boundaries. Of course *customs* vary from place to place and from generation to generation, but man's basic concept of right and wrong has been remarkably consistent. An amazing agreement, for example, that it is right to tell the truth, and wrong to kill someone for the fun of it, has characterized men and women over thousands of years and across hundreds of countries.

Some say that right and wrong are just words which describe what is good for society as a whole; that society has evolved these values over the years for its own preservation. There is, however, no historical evidence for this evolution and, what's more, we can ask, 'Why should society be preserved?' There are a number of reasons for this but they all end up at, 'it's right for human life to continue'. But who says it's right? We just know it is; and so we are back to our inner knowledge of right and wrong.

We don't leave it up to individuals to decide what is right and wrong, as though 'my view of right and wrong is just as good as yours' – for two reasons.

Firstly, it would result in chaos in the world. If you made up your mind to believe that it was right to make love to your neighbour's wife whenever you wanted to, drown his dog if you felt like it and break his children's legs for reclaiming the ball they had kicked into your garden, he may well feel that it was right to respond by shooting you in the head! No, if we all made up what was right and wrong as we went along, society would disintegrate in a matter of days.

And secondly, we know we would never accept this principle in practice; it just wouldn't work. If, in an argument with someone, you accuse them of lying to you they would usually put up a variety of defences – you misunderstood, circumstances have changed, you lied as well, and so on. But no one ever says, 'Of course I lied', assuming that would be quite acceptable. We may have double standards, we may lie all the time, but we *still expect other people* to tell the truth. People agree that this standard is right – a lie is wrong. Without this agreement no meaningful conversation is possible.

So we live all the time assuming that a real difference exists between right and wrong – we are not free to change them whenever we want to. If God didn't put the knowledge of good and evil there, who or what did?

Problems in the world

There's all the difference in the world between *knowing* what is right and *doing* it. And not many people seem to be doing it! Every night the TV brings news of the massive problems in the world – war, famine, terrorism, nuclear escalation and civil unrest. Even in the wealthy countries unemployment and inflation cause deprivation and despair, especially in many of our urban areas, which are fast becoming concrete wildernesses of hopelessnes and frustration. And what about the problems of family life? One in three marriages ends in divorce. Child abuse is more widespread than we dreamed possible and thousands of wives live in daily fear of physical and verbal violence. And we have problems as individuals: a rising suicide rate, vast increases in stress-related illnesses and a discovery of several new diseases (the best known is AIDS) which we simply have no idea how to cure.

This catalogue of problems shows what a fine mess we have got ourselves into. Why can't we get along together as individuals, families and nations? What can be done about it? Every political solution has been tried. The Old Mother Hubbards of national leadership search the political cupboard for answers in vain. It is empty. Down the centuries monarchies and republics, democracies and dictatorships (and everything in between) have failed to produce really just and fair societies. Economics, education, coercion and religion have all been explored in the search for some kind of answer. So far it's a pretty depressing story. We have managed to produce a world which spends a million pounds a minute on arms, while during the same minute thirty children die of starvation.

A simple illustration will help to show why Christians believe that all these human efforts are doomed to failure. Imagine seeing a pig in a pigsty and feeling that its manners left a great deal to be desired. All that snorting, slobbering over food and enjoyment of mud-rolling needs to be changed. We could burn the sty down and give the pig an antiseptic new home. We could make it such a luxurious pad that it would think it had died and gone to pig-heaven, or we could tell it we would start killing other pigs if it didn't mend its ways. Then again, it could be sent on a self-help course to improve its attitudes, or we could provide it with a private tutor to educate it and then give it the right to vote. All this would make it an affluent, clever, politically-aware pig with bags of self-confidence! But it is still a pig. A real pig. A pig with all its bad habits and as strong a desire as ever to roll in the mud.

Christians argue that this is precisely why all the usual answers to the human condition fail; they do not do anything to change the basic nature of people. They merely change our social and physical environment.

The Jesus message is this. People have got an inbuilt bias toward wrong. We know what the right thing to do is, but seem to have great difficulty doing it. A great Christian writer put it like this: 'I don't do what I would like to do, but instead I do what I hate . . . For even though the desire to do good is in me, I am not able to do it.'[8]

Jesus died to cancel out this bias, and all true Christians, while still having the bias, have a new power in their lives to correct it. Just as a brace controls crooked teeth by pulling against their natural direction, so when Jesus comes into our lives he acts as a brace bringing our crooked behaviour back into line. Slowly but surely he brings our actions into agreement with what he wants. The Christian solution, therefore, involves changes in our nature; deep changes, sometimes described as being 'born again'. This takes very seriously indeed our contribution to the trouble in the world, arguing that unless people are changed, the world never will be. Only a solution this radical will do. Everything else just scratches the surface.

The Jesus solution has implications for the world as a whole. Gordon Bailey's poem illustrates this:

Match of the Day

Mankind is but a football in a game that's played by fools,
With no effective referee to emphasise the rules.
Yet nailed upon a crossbar is a man, born for the role,
Whom stupid men have put to death, refusing his control.
So as a consequence one finds an anarchistic game,
Where death's a commonplace affair, and no one takes the
  blame.
Within the sunlit stadium, mankind gets kicked around;
His hopes and dreams, and high ideals, lie lifeless on the
  ground.
One commentator claims there isn't very long to play,
That most of those involved will be sent off on Final Day.
A starry universe spectates, and wonders at a sport,
Where man must fill his pen with blood, to write the match
  report!

Alexander Solzhenitsyn has repeatedly affirmed that he believes only Christianity is a radical enough moral force to bring sanity back to his country (Russia) and to the world. And bringing it right back to us as individuals, I have seen with my own eyes the revolutionary change brought about by knowing Jesus. Alcoholics, convicts, murderers and drug addicts – all completely different after an encounter with Jesus. And hundreds of ordinary men and women too, in whom the change is less dramatic but no less real. Christianity provides the only powerful solution to the needs of individuals and the planet as a whole.

Life, the universe and everything

Here I am on space-ship earth, spinning round at thousands of miles per hour and still managing to keep my breakfast down! What am I doing here on this small planet as it whirls through vast stretches of space? Why was I born?

Where am I going to end up? We can't live without some kind of answer to these questions – though thousands of the human race try to. They keep themselves busy with other things or push these thoughts to the back of their minds for another day. Like verbal boomerangs the questions keep coming back, demanding answers.

And the answers boil down to a choice between two stark alternatives. Either we are here for a purpose, or we aren't. We could be a great cosmic accident: a chance result of a haphazard evolutionary process begun at some point back in the mists of time. So our presence here on earth at the end of the twentieth century, our size, sex and personality, are just products of a chain of random coincidences. Our existence is one gigantic fluke. In recent years some scientists and philosophers have come to this conclusion. However, many of them have discovered that it is virtually impossible to live consistently with this idea. They end up by believing one thing in theory, while actually living as if the opposite were true. And no wonder, when you consider the mind-blowing implications of this theory. If I, and everything about me, is here by accident, a number of things follow. Presumably, if my brain is the end product of a random process, then the thoughts that come from it must ultimately have no significance. Words like *sense* and *nonsense* lose their meaning; they are only chemical impulses after all. Put simply, any theory that says that mankind is a product of chance has got an inbuilt destruct mechanism. If everything is a result of chance, then the theory itself is a result of chance, so why should I believe it?!

This kind of circular nonsense can be illustrated by a statement like 'all generalizations are false'. Now this can't possibly be true as a statement of fact. It has a 'self destruct' notice written all over it and as soon as we examine this phrase it explodes in our faces. If 'all generalizations are false' so is the generalization 'all generalizations are false' – then all generalizations are not false! Those who argue that we are just the result of a cosmic accident have to live with the tension of this illogically all the time.

The other problem with believing that we are here by accident is that it is not only illogical but also impractical. You can't live as though it were true, because it would mean that nothing really mattered as everything is the result of chance. If my feelings and beliefs aren't based on anything dependable and don't have any real significance, I might just as well be committed to a fire extinguisher as to my wife! But who can live like this? We all need things of significance in our lives (like family, friends and work) to give our existence meaning. Life would be unbearable without these things. If we are the result of a meaningless process, why do we cry out for meaning in our lives? I am afraid that the accident theory won't do.

The Christian would argue that there is a reason behind our existence, and a purpose for it. God created the human race (scientists can argue about how he did it) and gave it guide-lines for behaviour by way of the conscience and, of course, in the Bible. God has given deeper significance to some things than others; so we just know that the fire extinguisher is not to be valued in the same way as the wife. God wants us to enjoy his creation, respect our fellow humans and find real contentment in our lives. His goal for us is that we should receive his personal help to become like his son – the perfect human; a pretty amazing goal. All this gives real purpose to the Christian's life. Imagine a boat on a rough sea with dead engines, no captain, rudder or anchor. It would be blown about by the dictates of the wind and would drift at the whim of every passing current. Now imagine another boat in an equally bad storm. This boat has engine power and all its crew and equipment, plus a variety of maps and charts. This boat is going somewhere with both purpose and direction. Christians are glad to be in this second boat, and maintain that their choice is both logically consistent and practically workable. They would need some compelling reasons to abandon their views.

While we are thinking about the meaning of life we ought to think too about death. It's a frightening subject for many people, some of whom refuse to discuss it or hide their embarrassment by making a joke of it. Woody Allen speaks for most of us when he says, 'I'm not afraid to die. I just don't want to be there when it happens!' Death is life's final mystery, and we are going to need more than clever theories to face it with confidence. Christians know that Jesus has defeated death and that he has guaranteed a life of security and joy beyond the grave for them. Death becomes not an end but a beginning, not a brick wall but a doorway into another room. This is exactly what Jesus promised his followers:

'Do not be worried and upset . . . There are many rooms in my father's house, and I am going to prepare a place for you. I would not tell you this if it were not so.'

I have seen this theory working out in practice. I have conducted dozens of funerals, sat at lots of bedsides with dying people, spent hours counselling those who have been left behind. When the dying person was a committed Christian the whole experience is totally different. Of course there is sadness, anger, emptiness, and all the usual symptoms of grief, but there is some extra dimension which is present. It is almost impossible to explain, but there is hope, peace, even an element of joy in a truly Christian

113

funeral. When there is no faith, these elements are absent; and the whole process of grieving, and the funeral service itself, has a deep futility and hopelessness about it. And this is an issue we dare not make a mistake about. The most certain statistic of all is that one out of every one person dies! Have we got a philosophy of life which can cope with death; our own and those closest to us? Put coldly, and a little cruelly, will our beliefs stand up to the sight of our wife's corpse on a hospital bed, our child's coffin being carried into church or our father's casket disappearing for the last time behind the crematorium curtain? No one should answer 'yes' to that question without careful thought. I have known convinced atheists ask for God's help to cope with the loss of their partner, and others who have been angry at God for taking away someone they loved. And all without realizing the absurdity of being angry with (or asking for the help of) someone you don't believe exists!

In the face of the fact of death, most people simply look the other way and hope for the best. This is a strange response to life's most crucial question. We prepare financially by taking out insurances, we prepare practically by making a will; but we prepare spiritually by indulging in wishful thinking! Our eternal destiny deserves much more serious attention. And not just as a sterile academic exercise, but as a vital issue which affects us all. Those who come to terms with their own death stand a much greater chance of coming to terms with life. Most of us view death as going from the land of the living to the land of the dead. Christians have a marvellous assurance of a heaven in which all tears have been wiped away, and perfect rest and joy continue for ever. They are going *from* the land of the dying *to* the land of the living!

This chapter has attempted to look seriously at three very important questions – our sense of right and wrong, problems in the world, and the meaning of life. The Christian answers are perfectly rational. In two thousand years no one has come up with anything close to Christianity's practical, consistent world-view. No wonder Christians hold their views so passionately: they make sense and they work.

11
The final crunch

'I've made my mind up; don't confuse me with the facts!'
Lots of us act like this even if we don't use these precise
words. They explain why plenty of people are not Christians. The evidence in favour of Jesus Christ and his message
is very strong indeed. The purpose of this book has been
to show how compelling the facts really are. Sadly, few
people make decisions on the basis of facts! Most of us
operate at the level of feelings. Millions continue to smoke
despite the clear evidence that it damages your health. A
similar number overeat and take no exercise, even though
the problems associated with this kind of lifestyle are well
known. And even if you are a non-smoking, bran-eating,
fitness fanatic, you are still not safe! If we examine our
behaviour carefully, almost all of us will find that we make
some decisions and adopt a certain lifestyle on the basis
of something other than the true facts. Personal pleasure,
tradition, and a variety of other feelings influence us
strongly.

This means that it is perfectly possible to read all the way through a book like this, and to be convinced that it makes a lot of sense. You can see the logic of the arguments. You agree that there is a great deal of evidence to support real Christianity. *And you are probably not going to do anything about it!* It's for the same reason that the forty-a-day man puffs himself to an early grave. He knows the facts about smoking, but doesn't want to (or feels he can't) change. And even if the facts are forcefully and clearly presented on a brilliantly creative video with additional coloured brochures, we will only have succeeded in making our heavy smoker a superbly well-informed, perhaps slightly more miserable, heavy smoker! Only when he *wants* to change are we going to see any real action.

So why don't people who can see a lot of sense in Christianity, want to become Christians? Here are some of the main reasons.

Comfort

They can't be bothered. They are too comfortable to be disturbed. It's as simple as that. It would be too much effort to change, too much of an upheaval in their lives. These people have a sleeping sickness in their souls. They are permanently in that twilight zone between waking and sleeping, when the last thing you want to do is move!

But the fact is, such people are in great danger. Some scientists were doing experiments with frogs and they discovered that if you throw a frog into boiling water it leaps out promptly. If, however, you place the frog in cold water and gradually heat it up, you can boil it alive before it realizes what's happening! Many people are in a similar predicament. They are being lulled into a false sense of security, tragically unaware of the danger they are in. Too comfortable.

Our relative affluence doesn't help our apathy problem. Full stomachs, warm homes and comparative security tend to dull our senses to life's crucial questions. We are exposed to

endless trivial distractions—television, videos, hobbies, and all kinds of other leisure pursuits. These activities (while not wrong in themselves) can create an environment in which our minds are permanently cushioned against serious thought.

The trouble is, 'comfortable' may not mean 'safe'. Suppose you are on a luxury liner in one of the plushest suites, with sumptuous furnishings and delicious food – everything your little heart desires. This is the life! The trouble is, the ship is the Titanic! You may be very comfortable, but you are in danger. Every human being is on a collision course with God. We've all failed to obey his laws and abide by his rules. Christianity is the provision of a life-boat, an escape from the anger God feels towards the wrong in our lives. Jesus died in our place to give us this escape route. All other escape routes are dead ends.

However satisfied we may feel, *if Christianity is true we are in desperate danger*. Remember, the Titanic was supposed to be unsinkable!

117

Cowardice

Many people don't become real Christians because they haven't got what it takes. Guts! They are too concerned about what people might say. That they have 'got religion', 'joined the God squad', or generally taken leave of their senses. Christianity is hardly fashionable and certainly not the kind of thing any self-respecting person would want to admit to.

And this is true of the so-called rebellious younger generation. They may want to rebel against an older generation's values, but they are just as terrified of being out of step with their mates as anyone else. That's one of the reasons why, no matter which British town you happen to be in, the young people all look the same! For all of us, there is one group of people whom we are determined to please.

On my first day at secondary school, I turned up looking cherubic in my newly acquired uniform. The only problem was I had been sold the wrong tie by a careless shop assistant! I was teased mercilessly about it and spent most of the day with my head bowed as if in prayer. To make matters worse the tie I had been sold belonged to one of our great rival schools! I hated being the odd one out, ridiculed and laughed at.

Most of us can relate to this. We think the people at work, lads in the pub, friends at the club, members of the family, will all think us very odd if we suddenly announce that we have bcome Christians. We don't want to be the odd one out. We want to be accepted and well thought of. And there is pressure from wider society too. Anybody who is over-enthusiastic about anything (politics, conservation, religion, etc.) is thought of as a fanatic. The emphasis today is on 'live and let live', 'take it easy', and 'relax'. We are becoming so laid back we are close to being laid out! In addition, cynicism is rampant; and negative, destructive humour is the order of the day. We have become so sophisticated that we can poke fun at everything. In this atmosphere passionate commitment to anything is difficult; commitment to Christianity (with its old-fashioned image) almost impossible.

Many people are afraid to become Christians because they fear rejection from friends, and because of society's subtle pressure to appear sophisticated and chic. All of which means we have to stop all this rubbish about Christianity being a soft option, something for those who can't handle life in their own strength! It is tough being a Christian. So tough there is not much of it about. Any fool can mock Christianity, but it takes real courage to become a follower of Jesus Christ.

Of course the cynics will ridicule. They know the price of everything and the value of nothing. But behind the mask of twentieth-century sophistication are disfigured and tear-stained faces. No hope here, no lasting joy, no comfort, nothing to sustain during times of tragedy. How many promises the smiling eyes of the mask make! How little fulfilment! Cliff Richard discovered this for himself some years ago:

> 'It was a few years into my show business career when I first sensed a sort of incompleteness. I don't know how else to put it. It was as though there was something more to life, despite the fact that I had so much going for me. Certainly as much fame, fortune and popularity as any one person could handle. The girls screamed, hits came regularly, accountants were employed to cope with the income, but, despite all that, it didn't add up to satisfaction. When I went home and took off the public mask, which I guess we all wear some of the time, I still had to live with the real me. And although I don't suppose I was any worse – or any better, come to that – than the next bloke, I knew that success, fans and money were no compensation for being restless deep within myself.' (Cliff Richard, *Mine to Share*; Hodder.)

Cost

What will I have to give up if I become a Christian? Most people have a worry that becoming a Christian will involve them in not doing all the things they enjoy doing. Well, there is no getting away from the fact that Christianity is costly. It cost God's son his life and it's not going to cost us any less. We probably won't be called on to die physically for our faith, but we will be called on to 'die' to everything God doesn't want us to be. Being a Christian costs everything – you are not your own boss any more. What God wants is more important now than what you want.

All this can seem pretty terrifying until you examine what it is you are being called on to do. From the outside it looks like a raw deal: 'Give up wine, women and song and Christianity will give you stewed tea, elderly ladies and hymns!' No wonder the price of Christianity seems high. But this caricatured comparison misses the point. Why?

Firstly, we get something permanent to replace the temporary. The good feelings we get from the new gadget at home, our participation in sport, a favourite TV programme, are all passing pleasures; they are not going to last. Christianity offers something that can't be pushed out by the latest craze, replaced by any change in fashion, be made obsolete by any development in technology or be terminated by death! It puts the cost into perspective when you realize you will be giving up what you can't keep in order to accept what you can't lose.

Secondly, all other satisfactions are cheap imitations.
Why be satisfied with a print when you can have the original? It's very hard to explain this without sounding arrogant. Sometimes when I talk to people who are not Christians I am amazed at how little it takes to please them. What they describe as exciting appears to me to be unsatisfying and flat. Say a professor of mathematics was talking to a six-year-old about arithmetic. The professor would find it impossible to limit his thinking to addition and substraction when he had tasted the delights of calculus and geometric progression! Of course, he would understand the boy's position because he had been at that stage once himself. But he would gain little joy in attempting $16-7=?$ The boy, on the other hand, would think it a great accomplishment if he could solve this problem! If he saw

some of the professor's work, it would look like a page filled with a jumble of meaningless shapes. He would dismiss it as silly or boring; not half as good as the real numbers he was working with. In the same way, non-Christians generally do not understand what real Christianity is all about and so tend to dismiss it. Christians on the other hand, understand why non-Christians find some things so satisfying because they used to share their priorities. Since meeting Jesus, however, there is no way they could be satisfied with what appear now to be trivial pursuits!

Church

Noel Edmunds has said, 'The church is the dullest experience that we have in this country.' This is one of the main reasons why people are put off Christianity. TV often shows clergymen as fanatical bigots or wet, effeminate wimps who wouldn't harm a fly. Church congregations seem to consist mainly of elderly women. They meet in old buildings and participate in some obscure ritual called worship, which involves little more than entering the building, singing a few hymns and being asked to part with some of your hard-earned money to help prevent the steeple falling down. A club with three rules – turn up, sing up and cough up!

Sadly, some churches are like this. But they are (thank God) a dying breed. The real church is not a building but a people who have met Jesus. This church is completely different from its sick image. The true church of Jesus is growing rapidly. Two thousand new churches are started *every week* and five hundred thousand people are converted to Christianity during the same period! The only continent on which the church is not growing rapidly is Europe, but even here there are encouraging signs of life. I could take you to dozens of churches where the services are interesting, varied and exciting, and the atmosphere has to be experienced because it can't be explained. So don't be fooled by bad experiences you may have had – boring school assemblies, TV vicars, or the crusty old fool who did your gran's funeral. The church need not be like this. In fact, a real church isn't.

Even if Christianity is true, these four obstacles stand in the way of many people coming to accept the message for themselves. Comfort, cowardice, cost and the church's image can provide pretty strong opposition. And we have not mentioned the greatest opposition of all yet. It is an incredibly dangerous opponent for two reasons – it is immensely powerful and also a brilliant master of disguise. So superb is this disguise that most of the human race doesn't even realize it's there! This evil power operates on everyone and its main job is to blind people to the truth about themselves and God. Christians believe that this power is an evil personality called Satan. He has conned most of humanity into believing that he is either a figure of fun with a pitchfork in his hand, or a figment of the imagination. Unfortunately, he is real. He operates just like a deadly virus. You can't see him but the damage he does is terrible.

Unless you are aware of this power at work you will never understand why a decision to follow Jesus Christ is so hard to make. *Somebody does not want you to make it.* Imagine making a decision to take up serious jogging, but every time you were getting changed you were struck by a viral infection which made you very lethargic. It would take a massive effort of will to force your body out of the door and to start running.

Similarly, whenever people make a decision to examine the claims of Christianity seriously, Satan mobilizes his forces to produce 'spiritual lethargy'. 'When you're a bit older', he whispers; 'remember your image', 'no one believes it any more', and so his deceits go on. This is usually enough to keep us away from the discovery of God. How easily we are deflected from our search for truth! These excuses are going to sound really lame when we come face to face with God. 'Oh, sorry God; they told me you were dead. Anyway, I would have tried to find out about you but I was too busy. It just seemed irrelevant compared with following Manchester United!'

All sounds pretty sick really. 'Too busy'? – when the average person in Britain spends over eighteen hours a week watching the box! 'No one believes it any more'? – when there are seven times as many people in church on Sunday as were watching football on Saturday! No, these excuses don't bear up to examination. Someone is conning us!

So what?

Single-minded people make it to the top in sport, politics and just about any other field. They have to be single-minded to cope with the great pressures that they are under. Daley Thompson, Olympic champion in the decathlon, says:

> 'There are times during the long winter months when the monotony of that seven days a week training routine really brings me down. The public only see the glamorous side of it when you are racing to a glorious victory in front of a packed crowd or hitting the headlines as you break another record. What they don't see is the shivering athlete standing in the middle of the frozen wastes of Crystal Palace on a January afternoon trying to summon the enthusiasm to throw a shot which is so cold it sticks to the skin of your neck!'
> (Daley Thompson, *One is My Lucky Number;* WH Allen).

No one doubts this commitment to winning. If only we displayed half the commitment in our search for truth, many more people would find it.

Do we really want to know the truth about ourselves and our world? Do we really want to feel clean inside; set free from the mistakes of the past? Do we want to experience life as God intended? If so, we need to consider the offer that Christianity makes, very seriously. This will take some time and real commitment to the process of discovering, but the prize beats an Olympic Gold by miles!

So what now?

I am always very sceptical when I see books or articles with titles like 'Six Simple Steps to a Better Sex Life' or 'How to Earn a Million by a Week on Friday'! The kind of book that reduces a massive area of expertise down to a few simplistic steps which fail to do the subject justice. I hope to avoid being so naïve, but I have to give four steps which I believe can demonstrate to the honest enquirer the truth and power of Christianity.

1. Be bold!

Have the guts to examine all the evidence honestly, even if it makes you very uncomfortable. The motto of the SAS, 'Who dares wins', is nowhere more relevant than in the search for truth. People may well want to know what's come over you. The search could easily be difficult! Be bold enough to keep on searching even if you don't appear to be getting anywhere. Reject the weakness of many in our society whose motto appears to be, 'If at first you don't succeed – give up and try something else!'

Be strong enough to start the journey with as little excess baggage as possible. In other words, get rid of as many preconceptions and prejudices as you can. Don't decide Christianity is going to be false (or true) before you start. There are already too many people who make up their minds and then look round for facts to support their view – don't add to their number. If you can be ruthless enough with yourself, try to forget all you think you know about Christianity and approach the whole thing as if you'd never heard of it.

A great many important scientific discoveries have been made by using this 'clean sheet' principle. Ignoring what 'everybody knows', these scientists demonstrated the opposite to be true. Centuries ago 'everybody knew' that the earth was flat and that leeches were a good cure for many physical ailments. The fact was that everybody was wrong and was shown to be wrong when brave men stood against them with the facts. Most of us have grown up in a world which has made similar statements about Christianity, conditioning us against it. 'Everybody knows that the church is a dying institution.' 'Everybody knows that no intelligent person believes that stuff any more.' It is going to take a bold person to ignore 'everybody knows' and examine the evidence on its merits. This boldness is vital if we are to demonstrate that 'everybody' is as wrong today as when leeches could be bought at the chemist!

2. Be clear . . .

. . . about what the Christian faith is *not*. It is not about stopping swearing, giving up chocolate for Lent or becoming a fan of *Songs of Praise*. The Christian message is:

God exists. He caused the world to come into being, and created human life. This human life was given the freedom to follow God's laws or reject them. Mankind went its own way and has chosen to do so ever since.

God, because he is loving, wants to give his creatures another chance, so he came to earth as a human and took on himself the punishment for our rebellion. Then he offered this second chance to everyone who would accept it as a free gift.

The gift, when it is received, brings with it a guarantee of eternal happiness with God after death; forgiveness, peace and purpose on earth. The gift does not guarantee an easy life, free from trouble – sometimes precisely the opposite. Receivers of the gift expect opposition from natural and supernatural enemies. They also enjoy a new strength and enter a dimension of living which would otherwise be unknown.

3. Be active!

Say you wanted to find out about athletics. If you went to one race meeting as a spectator and then dismissed athletics as a waste of time – I'd say you weren't really bothered in the first place. You couldn't possibly dismiss the fun of competing, the sense of achievement in participating and the thrill of winning on the strength of this one brief view from the stands. Being an athlete, like Christianity, is not a spectator sport. Get out on the track and run, talk to some real athletes, chat to a coach, read some books on athletics, and then decide if it is for you. So, if you really want to find out if Christianity is true:

4. Start doing things real Christians do!
• *Get a Bible and begin to read the New Testament.* Make sure you have a modern translation. Find a Christian book shop and ask them to recommend one or two books which explain the Christian faith. If you find the Bible difficult to understand, they will have booklets which explain it bit by bit.

•*Go to a lively church.* Ask questions about everything in the service you don't understand. (It's usually best to wait until the end to do this – most churches aren't too happy with questions during the sermon!) Make an appointment to see one of the leaders. Be polite, but ask every awkward question about God that you really want to know the answer to. Don't try to ask clever questions just for the sake of an argument. A good leader will find it difficult to take you seriously if you do. Go to church regularly for a number of months. Keep asking questions. Keep asking yourself, 'Is this real? Is anything happening to me? Is it true?' (If you can't find a lively church near you, write to, or phone, the Evangelical Alliance and ask if they can tell you of one locally.)

•*Start to pray.* At first it will feel very odd talking into what seems like empty space, but it does get easier. You might want to start by praying something like,

'God, I'm not even sure that you are there; but if you are I want to find out the truth about you. Please show yourself to me so that I can find out for myself what you are really like.'

A prayer like this confirms that you are serious in your

126

search. Don't try to use religious language or pretend to be holy or pious. God already knows you aren't! Just talk as naturally as possible.

●*Be changed!* None of these steps will *make* you a Christian – they are stages along the road to discovery. Ultimately, being a Christian involves a relationship. A growing friendship with Jesus as a person. An experience of his love and power. This encounter with the living God is what real Christianity is all about. Don't settle for anything less. Don't settle for anything *else*. Don't settle – search! Then you will discover the truth of his promise for yourself:

> 'Then you will call to me. You will come and pray to me, and I will answer you. You will seek me, and you will find me because you will seek me with all your heart.'[10]

Sources of Bible quotations used in this book

1. John 14:6
2. Acts 4:12
3. Romans 6:23
4. Ephesians 2:8
5. Matthew 16:13–16 and John 20:24–28
6. John 10:33 (NIV)
7. From Matthew 23
8. Romans 7:15, 18
9. John 14:1–2
10. Jeremiah 29:12–13

To find out more

John Allan, **Sure Thing**; Kingsway.
Colin Chapman, **The Case for Christianity**; Lion Publishing.
Peter Cotterell, **This is Christianity**; IVP.
David Field and Peter Toon, **Real Questions**; Lion Publishing.
Michael Green, **World on the Run**; IVP.
C S Lewis, **Mere Christianity**; Fontana.
Josh McDowell, **Evidence that demands a verdict;** and **More evidence that demands a verdict;** Campus Crusade.